PUB W...
— IN —
Bedfordshire

THIRTY CIRCULAR WALKS
AROUND BEDFORDSHIRE INNS

James A. Lyons

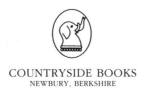

COUNTRYSIDE BOOKS
NEWBURY, BERKSHIRE

First Published 1994
© James A. Lyons 1994
Revised and updated 1996, 1999, 2002

COUNTRYSIDE BOOKS
3 Catherine Road
Newbury, Berkshire

ISBN 1 85306 319 3

Dedicated to
'Max'
for whom it proved to be a 'book too far'.

Designed by Mon Mohan
Cover illustration by Colin Doggett
Photographs by the author
Maps by S.R. Lyons

Produced through MRM Associates Ltd., Reading
Printed by Woolnough Bookbinding, Wellingborough

Contents

Publisher's Note

We hope that you obtain considerable enjoyment from this book; great care has been taken in its preparation. However, changes of landlord and actual closures are sadly not uncommon. Likewise, although at the time of publication all routes followed public rights of way or permitted paths, diversion orders can be made and permissions withdrawn.

We cannot of course be held responsible for such diversion orders and any inaccuracies in the text which result from these or any other changes to the routes, nor any damage which might result from walkers trespassing on private property. However, we are anxious that all details covering the walks and the pubs are kept up to date and would therefore welcome information from readers which would be relevant to future editions.

1 Yelden

2 Riseley

3 Little Staughton

4 Sharnbrook

5 Odell

6 Milton Ernest

7 Tempsford

8 Stevington

9 Turvey

10

11 BEDFORD

12 Wrestlingworth

13 Old Warden

14 Broom

15 Houghton Conquest

16 Pegsdon

17 Clophill

18 Ampthill

19 Ridgmont

20 Shillington

21 Woburn

22 Pulloxhill

23 Sharpenhoe

24 Wingfield

25 Milton Bryan

26 Linslade

27 Totternhoe

28 Dunstable

29 LUTON

30 Whipsnade

Area map showing locations of the walks.

Introduction

Bedfordshire is a largely agricultural county, which, in spite of its small size, offers considerable scope to walkers. When exploring this part of the English countryside we walk in the footsteps of those who have gone before us and familiarity often cloaks a county that has much to offer – and not a few surprises for those who undertake these particular pub walks.

In the south, the chalk downs of the Chilterns, where they extend into the county as far as Dunstable, and beyond as outcrops, provide excellent walking. A major river, the Great Ouse, with its tributaries the Ivel and Ouzel, meanders across the county and stretches of these rivers provide more relaxing walks, whilst, to the north, the farming uplands and more remote villages beckon.

A striking feature of the northern, upland part of the county is the reminders of World War II, from abandoned airfields to concrete tracks that lurk deep in the woods. Many pubs in this area of the county display wartime photographs or memorabilia from this era, and some still see regular reunions of those who were stationed in Bedfordshire at this momentous time.

World War II apart, every effort has been made to include routes that are interesting in their own right. To this end they not only visit some of the finest pubs in the county, but also cover the best areas for walking and in the process manage to incorporate most of the county's major tourist attractions.

Directions have been kept straightforward and are accompanied by sketch maps giving a simple yet accurate idea of the route to be taken. For those who like a more detailed map, the Ordnance Survey sheets are recommended and the relevant number in the OS Landranger 1:50 000 series is given. The walks are from 2½ to about 6 miles long and vary in difficulty according to the terrain covered. Some are easy, others quite demanding, especially in muddy conditions. At least two could be successfully completed by wheelchairs and pushchairs.

A stout pair of shoes is recommended as you are likely to encounter the odd patch of mud, even on the sunniest day – particularly on riverside paths and in the low-lying watermeadows of some of the walks. For this reason, a change out of muddy footwear before going into any pub might go a long way towards ensuring a warm welcome for subsequent walkers!

Due acknowledgement must be made to the work of the county's Leisure Services Department which is responsible for keeping open the network of field-paths, and the creation of circular and long distance walks. Parts of some of the 14 official circular walks in the county have been incorporated in the walks in this guide. In addition, stretches of the following long distance paths have also been included:

Greensand Ridge Walk (GRW) – 42 miles from Leighton Buzzard in the west of the county, to Gamlingay Cinques, just over the Cambridgeshire border.

Icknield Way Path – 120 miles. Connects the Ridgeway at Ivinghoe Beacon, Buckinghamshire, with the Peddars Way at Knettishall Heath, Suffolk. (See *Pub Walks along the Icknield Way Path*, by the writer of this book.)

The John Bunyan Trail – 70 miles. Circular walk within the county beginning and ending at Sundon Country Park on the Chiltern Hills.

The Kingfisher Way – 21 miles following the River Ivel in the east of the county.

The Three Shires Bridleway – 37 miles from Tathall End in Buckinghamshire to Grafham Water in Cambridgeshire.

All enquiries regarding the condition of public rights of way in the county, whatever their classification, should be made to the Definitive Map Section, Heritage and Countryside, Bedfordshire County Council, Cauldwell Street, Bedford MK42 9AP. Telephone: (01234) 228320.

Other long distance walks referred to in the text are The Grand Union Canal Walk, 145 miles from London to Birmingham, and the Clopton Way, mainly in Cambridgeshire, 11 miles from Gamlingay to Wimpole Hall.

As for the pubs that appear in the guide, they represent only a selection of possible choices, although the combination of good pub/beer/food/walk is not always easy to find. Many establishments may qualify on one or more counts, but far fewer satisfy all of them. Also, the necessity of an even, geographical spread across the county precluded pubs which otherwise would have appeared. These 30 pubs, however, offer a wide choice, from Victorian alehouses, with the beer dispensed direct from the cask in the cellar, to modern pubs serving traditional ales and 'pub grub' to up-market establishments with à la carte menus and a wine list to match. However much they differ, they all have one thing in common – a congenial, friendly atmosphere and a warm welcome.

Finally, the compilation and writing of this guide has been a cooperative endeavour, with my wife, Sally, drawing the maps and more than assisting at every stage of production. We walked many miles together looking for the best pub walks – we hope that you gain as much enjoyment from walking them as we did.

Cheers!

James A. Lyons

1 Yelden
The Chequers

Well known for its large motte and bailey earthworks, this upland village in its rural setting has some attractive thatched cottages and farmhouses. The original Chequers survived a fire and was substantially re-built in the 1950s. A plain, red-brick building, it has built up a loyal following locally and provides a warm welcome in comfortable but unfancy surroundings.

In addition to the long bar-room with its large open fireplace, there is a games room and a separate dining area. Meals are all home-made with over 30 main courses on offer, including very popular pies. Vegetarian dishes and children's portions are available. The main bar area is plainly but pleasingly furnished and has a notable wall display relating to the USAAF 305 (Can Do) Bomb Group, who walked across the fields from the nearby airfield at Chelveston (Northamptonshire) to drink here during the war. The Chequers is a freehouse currently serving Fuller's London Pride, Batemans XB plus two guest real ales. Draught Guinness, cider and three lagers are also available. A good wine list complements the comprehensive menu of home-cooked food. There is a garden and children's play area to the rear of the pub.

Dogs are welcome but restricted to the garden when the bar gets crowded.

On Mondays and Tuesdays the pub is closed lunchtimes and open from 5.30 pm to 11 pm. Wednesday to Friday it opens from noon to 2.30 pm and 5.30 pm to 11 pm. Saturdays noon to 11 pm and Sundays noon to 10.30 pm.

Telephone: (01933) 356383.

How to get there: Yelden is 2 miles east of Rushden (Northamptonshire), on the Bedfordshire side of the border. From the A6(T) Bedford to Rushden road turn off to Newton Bromswold and Yelden, or turn off the A45 Kimbolton to Higham Ferrers road at Chelveston, if approaching from the north.

Parking: There is a car park in front of the pub.

Length of the walk: 5½ miles. OS map Landranger 153 Bedford, Huntingdon; Explorer 225 Huntingdon and St Ives (GR 013668).

A walk across high, farming uplands, linking the villages of Yelden and Melchbourne. Yeldon itself has extensive motte and bailey earthworks to explore, whilst Melchbourne, at the halfway stage, has some very photogenic thatched cottages.

The Walk

From the pub the route turns left, along the High Street. Where the road bends right, it keeps ahead along a concrete farm track, following the line of the Three Shires long distance bridleway. A few hundred yards along this track the walk leaves the Three Shires Way and turns left on a bridleway behind two large barns. Once clear of the barns and farmyard clutter, a headland track follows the hedge up a long rise, with good views behind, across the valley.

In the top corner of this large arable field, the path turns left, through a narrow belt of trees, on the other side of which it bears left, along another headland track. Across the field to the right can be seen the farm buildings of Crowfield Farm. When the walk has drawn level with the front of these buildings, it turns at right angles, heading across the crop. This field-path is a right of way shown on the OS Pathfinder map, although it is not waymarked or indicated across the crop by the farmer.

Past the front of the farm buildings, the route bears right, across a track, then left, on a good track to the left of the farmhouse. From here the track winds left and right across high, arable uplands. After crossing a footbridge, it keeps to the right of a small wood, beyond

9

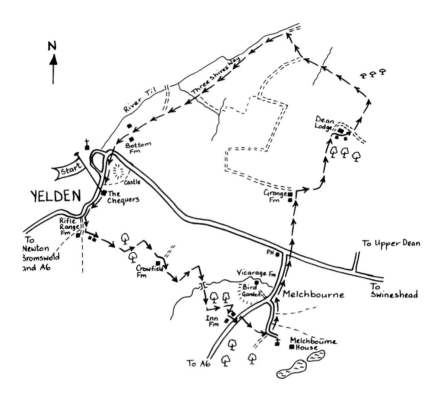

which it turns right, and then left, to run through the farmyard of Inn Farm and meets the road. Here the route turns left, along the road for a few yards, and then right, down a bank to follow a headland path. At the top corner of the field, the path is fenced-in as it runs between houses to emerge on a track, along which it turns left to a cul-de-sac leading to Melchbourne House and the village church.

The church of St Mary is flanked on either side by two unusual, three storey, thatched houses. To the left of one of these is Melehbourne House, where, on 21st July 1944, the famous wartime Glenn Miller band gáve a concert for over 1,000 American servicemen stationed in this area. To the right of the church is a long row of very pretty thatched cottages, built by the St John family in the first half of the 18th century for estate workers.

The walk turns left on the roadside path past the cottages, after which it continues to a T-junction. Here it turns right to follow the road uphill, then down to another T-junction. Over the road it follows a drive leading up and through the farmyard belonging to Grange Farm.

At the T-junction, the walk turns right and follows the road uphill, then down to another T-junction, with the St Johns Arms pub on the left. Here, the route crosses straight over the road and takes the farm drive ahead, leading up to and through the farmyard belonging to Grange Farm. At the T-junction behind the farmyard the route turns right along a good track which is followed for about a mile across wide, arable fields on farming uplands. The track bends left, then down and up a shallow valley, past a wood on the right to the top of the rise. Soon, the right of way turns right, between the swish buildings of Dean Lodge Farm, complete with stables and ornamental well. Clear of the buildings the track bears ahead, slightly to the left and up another rise, from the top of which there is a panoramic view north and west across rolling farmlands. The wireless mast in the middle distance, with what looks like a surviving hangar at its base, marks the site of Chelveston, home to the B 17 Flying Fortresses of the 305th Bomb Group, USAAF, under the command of Colonel Curtis 'Iron Ass' Le May during World War II.

The track bears left as it runs downhill before crossing a bridge over a ditch from where it continues ahead for some distance. Where the track turns left, the walk keeps ahead across an arable field aiming to the left of a large willow tree in the hedge on the opposite side. Through the hedge it turns left, back again on the waymarked Three Shires Way. The track continues ahead between high bushes and trees, with the narrow river Til on the right, before reaching open, level countryside. The tower of Yelden church can be seen in the distance ahead to the right and, eventually, the track is tarmaced as it runs into the outskirts of the village.

At the road the walk continues ahead passing the prominent mounds of the motte and bailey earthworks on the left and attractive, thatched cottages on the right. Past the corrugated village hall (to the right of which a footpath leads to the earthworks), the walk arrives back at the pub, opposite which stands a thatched cottage with a ploughing scene painted on its gable end.

Riseley
The Fox and Hounds

2

Riseley is a mainly brick-built village, as brick making was a local industry dating back to the 16th century. There are also a number of timber framed houses, three of which now form the spacious and very comfortable accommodation provided by the Fox and Hounds. Three heavily beamed, open-plan areas correspond roughly with the ground plan of the original houses. Furniture and furnishings border on the luxurious and even the carpeting is interesting with its fox and hounds theme – spot the fox in each bar! A single, long bar has a cold cabinet at one end which displays the fresh steaks for which the pub is famous. Diners make their own selection from a wide choice and the steak is then grilled to their preference on an open grill in one of the dining areas. That the pub's reputation for its steaks has spread far and wide can be seen by the letter of appreciation and presentation clock from the veterans of the 2003 Ordnance Squadron, USAAF, who hold reunions here and were stationed in the area during the war. In addition to steaks, there is a good à la carte menu which changes daily and always includes vegetarian dishes. Meals are served seven days a week, but steaks are not available on Saturday lunchtimes.

The Fox and Hounds is a Charles Wells pub and serves their Eagle

IPA and Bombardier Best Bitter, plus a guest beer which changes from time to time. Draught lager and Guinness are also available and during the summer there is usually an extra real ale. A comprehensive wine list is on offer. A terrace to the rear of the pub provides an ideal location for al fresco meals during the summer.

Opening times are Monday to Saturday 11.30 am to 2.30 pm and 6.30 pm to 11 pm, and on Sunday from noon to 3 pm and 7 pm to 10.30 pm.

Telephone: (01234) 708240.

How to get there: Riseley is about 6 miles north of Bedford, between the A6(T) and the B660. The pub is in the High Street at the centre of the village.

Parking: There is a large car park to the front and one side of the pub.

Length of the walk: 5 miles. OS map Landranger 153 Bedford, Huntingdon; Explorer 225 Huntingdon and St Ives (GR 040627).

A walk which follows tracks across arable farmland and includes good views from the higher ground to the north-west of the village. Also, the discovery that more than just crops were once planted in this pleasant countryside!

The Walk

From the pub the route turns left along the road. After a short distance, it turns right, across a bridge over a roadside stream. From here it follows Gold Street up a rise, at the top of which it turns left along Rotten Row. On the outskirts of the village, opposite the last house on the left, it turns right on a farm drive and bridle track, signposted to Lodge Farm.

Just before the farm, the route turns off on the right-hand verge, shortly before reaching an open gateway. The path then stays to the right of the farmhouse and runs alongside a red-brick barn, keeping to the edge of the arable field. Past the farm, a track is crossed next to an ash tree, and the route continues ahead, keeping to the left of the hedge with wide views across open farmland. Where the hedge ends, the path continues ahead along a raised bank. In the corner of the field it dog-legs left and then right, before running uphill to join a surfaced drive in front of a house on the right. The route turns right, along the drive which leads to the farmyard and house belonging to Haring's Farm. Past the front of the third large barn on the right, the route turns right, along a concrete track.

The route stays with the main track as it runs ahead and through dense, mainly coniferous woodland, ignoring turn offs and curious

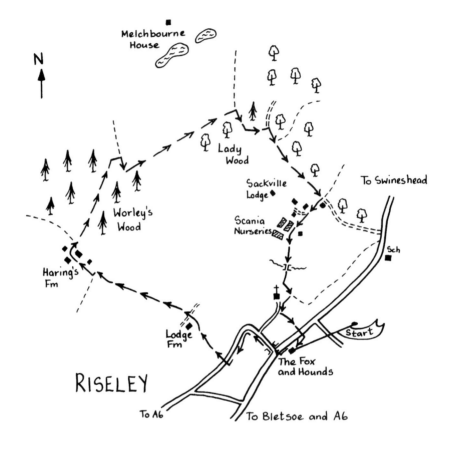

N

Melchbourne House

Lady Wood

To Swineshead

Sackville Lodge

Scania Nurseries

Worley's Wood

Sch

Haring's Fm

Lodge Fm

RISELEY

Start

The Fox and Hounds

To A6

To Bletsoe and A6

looking 'laybys'. The dense cover afforded by the wood provides a sanctuary for wildlife, and deer are commonly seen in this area. After following the track for about ¼ mile, the edge of the wood is reached, where the route turns right, along a track. After about 50 yards or so, it bears left at an oak post and follows a field track along the top of the ridge, with good views across open country on either side.

To the north can be seen Melchbourne House, set in parkland and built as the home of Lord St John around 1610, now converted into apartments. During World War II, it was the HQ of the 8th Air Force Ordnance Depot – which explains the extensive network of old concrete tracks in this area and, perhaps, the pub's connections with the 2003 Ordnance Squadron. On 21st July 1944, the famous Glenn

Miller Band played an open air concert in front of Melchbourne House to over 1,000 American servicemen.

Where the track meets the left-hand corner of Lady Wood, it goes through a swing-gate and follows the edge of the wood before turning right on another bridle track. Shortly, the first of a network of concrete tracks is picked up and followed down to a T-junction. From here the route turns right and then runs downhill past overgrown laybys and tracks leading off into the woods.

Progress down this track reveals many signs that point to the wartime use of this area as a huge bomb and ammunition dump supplying nearby American bases, such as Thurleigh. The temporary buildings and bunkers have long since disappeared, but the network of concrete tracks survives to remind walkers of less peaceful times. One can only guess at what memories these woods and tracks must hold for the men who armed the B17 'Flying Fortresses' and cheered the Glenn Miller Band at nearby Melchbourne House.

Eventually the walk leaves the track ahead and turns right along a drive leading to a farm and nurseries. Where the drive turns right the right of way continues ahead across a small paddock before running between a new house and the end of the glasshouses. Over a stile in the corner it bears left, across a sheep pasture, keeping roughly in line with the distant church tower. Over a new fence and then right, across a footbridge, it crosses an arable field, on the other side of which it turns left on a path leading to the rear of the church.

Through a white swing-gate, a path is followed to the front of the church – keep an eye open for the lively corbel heads and gargoyles. From the church, the route runs down the lane for a short distance before turning left, down the side of an attractive black and white, thatched cottage. From here a metalled path leads down and across Ross Meadow newly restored to the local community for use as allotments and a small park. Eventually a footbridge over a small stream leads to the road along which the walk turns right, back to the pub.

③ Little Staughton
The Crown Inn

A village that straggles so close to the Bedfordshire/Cambridgeshire border that its church is only just in Bedfordshire, whilst most of nearby ex-RAF Little Staughton airfield is in Cambridgeshire. The present pub was largely rebuilt to replace the previous half-timbered and thatched building that suffered a disastrous fire in the early 1970s.

Comfortable accommodation is provided by settles and individual tables in a roomy, open-plan area served by an L-shaped bar. A large inglenook fireplace survives from the original building which, during the Second World War, was the 'local' for the elite Pathfinder Squadrons from the nearby airfield. Today, photographs and a Roll of Honour commemorate the men of 582 (Lancaster) and 109 (Mosquito) Squadrons, who still hold reunions in the pub from time to time.

The Crown Inn serves a good selection of bar snacks and traditional pub food. It is a free house and currently offers Greene King IPA, Fuller's London Pride, Morland Old Speckled Hen, Tetley Smooth Bitter and a guest ale. Guinness, cider and lager are also available on draught. There is a large garden to the rear of the pub.

16

The opening times are Monday to Friday from noon to 3 pm and 5 pm to 11 pm, Saturday from noon to 11 pm, and on Sunday from noon to 10.30 pm.
Telephone: (01234) 376260.

How to get there: Little Staughton is 7 miles north of Bedford, on the eastern side of the county, just on the Bedfordshire side of the border. The village lies between the B660 Bedford to Kimbolton road, and the A45 St Neots to Kimbolton road. The pub is at the northern end of the village, which is known as Green End.

Parking: There is a car park in front of the pub.

Length of the walk: 4 miles. OS map Landranger 152 Bedford, Huntingdon; Explorer 225 Huntingdon and St Ives (GR 102632).

This walk includes fine upland views, from the ridge outside the village, across a rolling, mainly arable landscape. To the north-west can be seen the village of Great Staughton whilst to the south, on a parallel ridge, is the main runway and hangars of ex-RAF Little Staughton, from where the Lancasters and Mosquitos of the famous Pathfinder Squadrons operated during World War II. Although only formed just over a year before the war ended, the award of two posthumous VCs bears testimony to the gallantry of the crews who flew over 2,000 bombing and target-marking sorties from here.

The route passes the site of extensive, manorial earthworks, then descends from the ridge and follows a stream, before returning to the pub by field-paths.

The Walk
From the car park in front of the pub the route turns right, along the road, for the short distance up to the T-junction. Here it turns right again, on the roadside path up the hill, past a lion-headed standpipe, common to all the villages in this part of the county. Just before the crest of the hill is reached, it turns left, along Church Lane leading to St Margaret's church, which is sited outside the village on the line of the ridge. The route continues to follow the lane, which becomes an unsurfaced farm-track after the church, as it crosses the Bedfordshire/Cambridgeshire border. Ahead to the right on ground slightly below the level of the ridge, glimpses can be caught of old war-time hangars that once sheltered the Pathfinder Mosquitos and Lancasters.

Further along the route passes a waymarked oak post as it keeps ahead and to the left of the substantial medieval earthworks which stand out prominently from the surrounding arable fields.

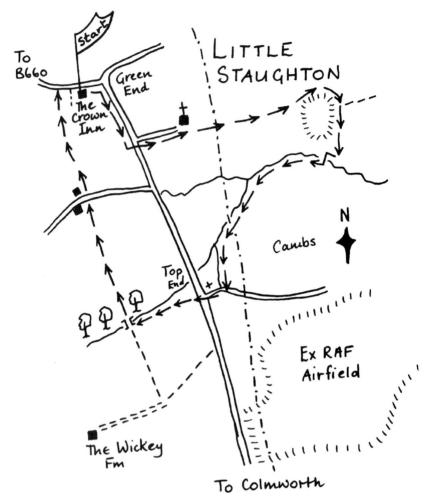

Known as Old Manor Farm, this banked and ditched rectangular site is extensive enough to enclose other mounds and a circular enclosure within its obviously defensive boundaries. The route keeps ahead to the end of the earthworks, where it turns right, close to the inner moat. From here it runs past a small causeway over the moat and continues downhill at the bottom corner to another oak post, where it turns right, over a ditch. Now it continues ahead to clip the bottom corner of the field as it runs in front of a small plantation of newly planted trees. It then turns left, over a newish footbridge across quite a large stream.

18

Over the footbridge, the route turns right along a headland track which follows the left-hand bank of the stream for a good ½ mile and crosses back into Bedfordshire. Eventually, another waymarked oak post next to a small, brick bridge or culvert marks the line of the path, which from here keeps to the left of a deep ditch, up to a road. Here the route turns right on the road, which runs down to a T-junction.

To the right of the T-junction is a tiny, disused chapel, complete with its crowded graveyard into which fresh graves are still being squeezed. This is Top End, the southernmost extremity of Little Staughton. Like many villages, it consists of a number of 'Ends', which have developed quite some distance from the original centre. The Crown is at Green End and the village also has a West End.

Across the road a finger-post indicates where the walk continues ahead on a field path to the left of a garden hedge. Over the field it crosses a footbridge then another field in the corner of which it turns right, over another footbridge. On the other side of the belt of trees a track keeps ahead to the left of a high hedge. Over a rise, it continues in the same direction before eventually bending to the left. Here the walk leaves the track to follow a footpath which crosses another footbridge before leading to the road.

Across the road, the route follows a bridleway to the right of a garden hedge which soon becomes a sunken track running between high banks and hedges. The track keeps ahead running slightly downhill and can be muddy during winter months or prolonged spells of wet weather. At the road the walk turns right, along the roadside path, back to the pub.

If time permits, when driving to or from this walk, visit the roadside memorial to the Pathfinder Squadrons located on the road to the south of Little Staughton. The granite memorial stands in a lay-by next to what was once the main entrance to the wartime airfield, now an industrial estate. Apart from the hangars referred to on the walk, much still survives including the runway and the wartime control tower.

Sharnbrook
4
The Swan with Two Nicks

Sharnbrook is a very pleasant village, with more than its fair share of attractive buildings. Limestone and thatch cottages from the 17th and 18th century, interspersed with houses of red brick, line the High Street on which the Swan with Two Nicks is also situated. The pub's name is derived from the annual 'swan-upping' when the swans of the river Thames have their beaks nicked to denote ownership – those of the Dyers' and Vintners' companies (Licensed Victuallers) being marked with two nicks.

The pub has two separate bars providing comfortable accommodation, with a dining area off the open-plan lounge. The lounge bar is all the cosier in winter for its open fire and, more unusually, has on display a 9 ft wooden propeller, thought to be from a First World War RE7. The menu and chalkboard specialities between them provide a wide choice of traditional, home-made meals, ranging from soups to stews, chillis to Sunday roasts, with Yorkshire puds in a class of their own! Vegetarian dishes are available and there is a children's menu. Meals are not served on Sunday evenings, unless by prior arrangement. The Swan with Two Nicks is a Charles Wells pub and offers four cask ales. Wells Eagle IPA, Bombardier, Adnams Broadside and Morland Old

Speckled Hen. Also available on draught are Mansfield Riding Mild, Guinness, Murphy's, two draught ciders and three lagers. Dogs are welcome in the public bar if it is not too crowded. There is a patio area to the rear of the pub, a pleasant, sheltered spot on fine days.

The opening times are Monday to Friday from 11.30 am to 3 pm and 5 pm to 11 pm. Saturday from 11 am to 11 pm, and on Sunday all day from noon to 10.30 pm.

Telephone: (01234) 781585.

How to get there: Sharnbrook is 6 miles north-west of Bedford and 4 miles south of Rushden. It lies just west of the A6(T), with the pub on the High Street near its centre.

Parking: There is a small car park to the left of the pub plus another just off the High Street.

Length of the walk: 6 miles. OS map Landranger 153 Bedford, Huntingdon; Explorer 208 Bedford and St Neots (GR 996596).

A walk with much of riverside interest along the Great Ouse between Sharnbrook and Odell. It also includes the village of Felmersham with its impressive church and passes by Felmersham Gravel Pits, a Site of Special Scientific Interest (SSSI) and nature reserve. Strong footwear advisable.

The Walk

From the pub the route turns right, along the High Street. Some way down the street it takes the second turning on the right, Normans Road, opposite the old Baptist chapel. It forks left after a few hundred yards along this road, where a fingerpost indicates a fenced-in footpath. Where the path ends, the route keeps ahead, over a stream, then to the left of a hedge, along a headland path. As progress is made along this path there are glimpses of the river and lakes to the left, along the bottom of the valley. Down a dip, the route keeps ahead over a cross-tracks, after which it meets the road at the top of the rise. Here it turns right, along the roadside verge, and up to the top of another rise, where it turns left along a track waymarked for the circular walk.

Past storage tanks on the right, the track keeps ahead over an arable field, heading towards Odell church, seen in the distance. On the other side of the field, the route turns right, on a wide, grassy track. A gap in the corner takes the track along the edge of another field, at the top corner of which, through another gap, the route turns left along a bridletrack. This track runs for some distance along the bottom of three large arable fields and there are wide views across the

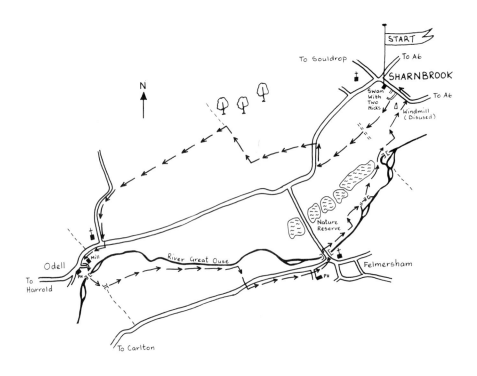

Ouse valley to the south. Eventually, the track meets a narrow lane, along which the route turns left. As the lane runs downhill, it passes the thatched farmhouse of Croft Farm with its old oak door, followed, on the other side of the road, by The Rectory and the 15th century church of All Saints.

Local legend has it that one of the barons of Odell sold his soul to the devil but sought sanctuary in this church when the day of reckoning came. Five marks on the porch are said to bear witness to the devil's frustrated fury. The dead baron's ghost is doomed to rise from the grave every hundred years and ride a desperate race once more to seek sanctuary in the church. Peter Bulkley, rector of the church from 1620 to 1635, followed the Pilgrim Fathers to the New World, where he founded the town of Concord, Massachusetts.

Past the church, the lane emerges at a T-junction on the outskirts of the village of Odell. Here the route turns right, up and over a small hill and then follows the road almost down to the Bell, an attractive pub, built of stone and thatched. Just before the pub is reached, the route turns left, along Mill Lane. Past an attractive row of sympathetically restored/converted small houses, the lane ends in front of the old mill, from where a path leads past a sluice gate to a footbridge across the river Great Ouse, a wonderful spot for photographs or from which to just enjoy the view. During the summer, the pub is also accessible from here via the gardens and car park.

On the other side of the river, a track is followed ahead across rough pasture to a gate. A short distance after the gate, the route turns left, over a footbridge and stile and continues along a path to the left of a stream and hedge. Across these pastures, where the hedge ends, the path carries on across the gap to a stile, beyond which it bears left, down to the river bank. The river is followed as far as the next hedgerow, where a double stile and footbridge is crossed and the route turns right. From here a fenced-in path runs to the next stile, after which it follows the fence across another pasture to a roadside stile in the corner. Here the route turns left, uphill for a good distance and then along a level stretch of road running parallel with the river below. After about ¼ mile, the road runs downhill into Felmersham.

If time permits, it is worth walking up the small hill from the bridge for a closer look at the fine west front of the church. Inside, there is much of interest, and a leaflet is available on a guided walk round the village.

Just before the bridge two seats placed here in 1977 to commemorate the Silver Jubilee make a pleasant resting place, after which the route turns left, over the five-arched stone bridge across the river. On the other side, the route turns right, along the river bank. After a good distance it leaves the river and turns left, through a swing-gate, to follow a fenced-in path across wide pastures. Having crossed the second of two concrete footbridges, it turns right, along a broad, grassy area in front of Felmersham Gravel Pits. These lakes are managed by the Bedfordshire and Cambridgeshire Wildlife Trust as a nature reserve. A network of paths within the reserve gives access to the lakes which, together with the nearby river, provide an important refuge for wildlife.

Where the gravel pits end, the route goes through a swing-gate, to follow a headland track to the right. At the corner a path ahead across the crop can be taken but it is easier to stay with the headland track, especially in wet weather or after ploughing. In the corner, the track turns left, along the edge of the field, which it leaves at a stile on the right. From here a broad, grassy track runs past a disused windmill, now converted into a glass topped look-out, complete with weather-vane. Eventually, the track arrives at the bottom of Sharnbrook High Street, where the route turns left, back up the street to the pub.

Odell
The Bell

5

Odell's riverside setting and proximity to the lakes of the Country Park has made it popular with summertime visitors, whilst the Bell's reputation for good beer and food has provided the village with an additional, year-round, attraction. Thatched and built of the local limestone, the interior has been extended to incorporate the old cellar and is now spacious enough to accommodate five bars or areas, all of which are much in demand in this very popular pub. One long bar serves all the areas, each of which has its own character. One with settles is preferred by the locals, whilst another, to the rear, is provided for families with children. There are many old beams, a huge inglenook fireplace, plus two other open fires, cosy in winter. The bars are all comfortably furnished and decorated in a traditional manner, providing that special ambience that characterises a real English country pub. There is a pleasant riverside garden to the rear, complete with a small aviary and Lucy, resident nosey-parker and guard-goose (confined to quarters during opening times). Dogs are welcome in the garden, but not in the bar areas.

The balance between good beer and good food is just about right, with the emphasis on real ale and home-cooking. The menu provides a choice of over a dozen main courses, including vegetarian dishes, plus chalkboard 'specials', including home-made curries and pies. To round off the meal there is a delicious selection of sweets, including 'Boozey Chocolate Mousse', made with Grand Marnier and brandy. Meals are not served on Sunday nights during the winter. The Bell is a Greene King house and serves their IPA, Rayments and Abbot Ale. Draught Guinness, cider and three lagers are also available.

The opening times are Monday to Saturday from 11 am to 2.30 pm and 6 pm to 11 pm, and on Sunday from noon to 3 pm and 7 pm to 10.30 pm. Open all day at the weekends during the summer.

Telephone: (01234) 720254.

How to get there: Odell is between Harrold and Sharnbrook, just 5 miles north-west of Bedford. It is best reached by turning off the A6(T) Bedford to Rushden road at Milton Ernest, if approaching from the south, or via Sharnbrook, if coming from the north.

Parking: There is a car park to the rear of the pub.

Length of the walk: 2½ miles. OS map Landranger 153 Bedford, Huntingdon; Explorer 208 Bedford and St Neots (GR 965577).

An easy stroll on good paths to the attractive village of Harrold and back again, via the lakes in the wildlife-rich Country Park. Most of this route is accessible to wheelchairs and pushchairs. As the Park includes the watermeadows between the lakes and the river Great Ouse, this walk can be extended to include the path round the small lake, or nature sanctuary, and/or the length of the river bank within the park.

The Walk
From the pub the route turns left, along Horsefair Lane. At the bottom of the lane a swing-gate gives access to the Country Park, through which the main path continues ahead between the lakes (ignore the path on the right).

The park is owned by Bedfordshire County Council and located between the villages of Harrold and Odell. Of the 144 acres, about half is water and the lakes and watermeadows provide a refuge for birds, of which over 160 different species have been recorded. They are also rich in wild flowers and attract a large number of butterflies. Dogs must be kept on a lead at all times in the park.

The path runs between a large lake on the right, and a smaller one on the left which is used as a nature sanctuary. After the sanctuary, the path continues for some distance before passing a lakeside bird hide on the right. From here the larger lake is screened by bushes and trees

25

for a few hundred yards before an overflow car park area is reached.

Here a grassy area, complete with picnic tables, runs down to the lake's edge on the right and 100 yards or so further on there is a lakeside telescope for bird-spotting. On the other side of the path there is a good view across the water of Chellington church, all that remains of a village decimated by the Black Death. Survivors of the plague burnt their houses to prevent the spread of infection and sought sanctuary in the church until the danger had passed. The village was rebuilt on a nearby site, now known as Carlton, and, after being virtually abandoned, the old church is back in use during the summer months as a church youth-hostel.

Further along, the path crosses a cattle grid after which it reaches the main car park opposite the visitors' centre which is open in the afternoons from April to September, and at weekends and bank holidays only, during the rest of the year.

Past the visitors' centre, the route leaves the park by the main entrance and turns left along the road for a short distance to view the bridge and causeway, part of which dates back to the 14th century. The bridge and foot causeway have a total of no less than 35 arches. Traffic is controlled by lights, making it possible for adventurous pedestrians to cross, using the recessed bays provided for this purpose in the days when the only traffic was horse drawn.

From the bridge the walk turns back along the road and left, along Hall Close. At the end of the close it forks right, past the front of St Peter's church. The church dates mainly from the 13th century and the remains of a priory of nuns attached to it in the middle ages lies under the area of Hall Close.

About 50 yards past the church, the route turns left at a crossroads where an oak post marks the continuation of the circular walk route. At the end of this path the route diverts left, between concrete bollards. At the small back lane it turns left again, down to the river bank for an excellent view of the old mill, complete with mill race – the second mill on this walk, the other being behind the Bell where the walk started.

Returning to the main route, the path continues ahead to the village green, with its circular stone lock-up of 1824 and octagonal 18th century market house or butter cross. The green is faced by attractive buildings, with a picturesque row of thatched cottages along its eastern side. Across the green, the walk turns left along the High Street, through the centre of the village. Just before the Oakley Arms, it turns right along a metalled path which follows a stream running behind the houses and shops. The path provides a fascinating glimpse of back gardens and streets as it runs through this built up area, passing everything from small factories to a farmyard within yards of the

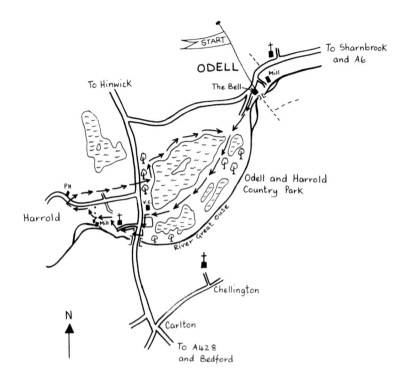

High Street.

Across Dove Lane, the path continues ahead and eventually meets the road opposite a side entrance to the Country Park. Over the road, the path runs through the park and down to the lake, where it turns left along the lakeside path. The path continues to follow the other side of the lake walked on the outward leg, to finally arrive back at the entrance to the park used earlier. From here, the route turns left and is retraced, back to the pub.

It is worthwhile continuing the walk down Mill Lane, just past the Bell. Beyond a row of attractive cottages is the old mill, past which a path leads to a footbridge over the river Great Ouse. The view from the bridge is enchantingly photogenic and during summer months there is easy access from here, across the mill leet, to the garden at the rear of the pub.

27

6 Milton Ernest
The Queen's Head

The Queen's Head is a 16th century coaching inn at the centre of this small village on the A6(T), north-west of Bedford. Within the last few years it has been extended and now operates as an hotel, a change which has not altered its traditional role as a village pub, popular with both locals and tourists. The original building is of local stone, whilst inside there are two separate, spacious bars. The wall of the lounge bar is decorated with a small version of the American 'Stars and Stripes' together with photographs of Glenn Miller, who, with his band, was based in Bedford in 1944. The famous wartime band leader used this pub as his 'local' when attending nearby Milton Ernest Hall, HQ of the USAAF Service Command. There is a dining area off the lounge bar, known as Miller's Restaurant, and a full à la carte menu is available, including vegetarian dishes, and a children's menu. Bar food changes daily and is displayed on a chalkboard. The restaurant prides itself on its home-cooking, and the home-made pies and soups are particular favourites of the regulars. Since it is also a hotel, food is available seven days a week. Outside is a small patio. Well-behaved dogs are welcome in the public bar.

The Queen's Head is a freehouse currently serving Charles Wells

Eagle IPA and Hall and Woodhouse Badger Best Bitter. Draught Guinness, lager and cider are also available.

The opening times are Monday to Saturday all day and on Sunday from noon to 3 pm and 7 pm to 10.30 pm.

Telephone: (01234) 822412.

How to get there: Milton Ernest is 4 miles from Bedford on the A6(T). The pub is on the main road, in the centre of the village.

Parking: There is a large car park to one side of the pub.

Length of the walk: 5 miles. OS map Landranger 153 Bedford, Huntingdon; Explorer 208 Bedford and St Neots (GR 018560).

This is an upland walk to Twinwood airfield, from where Glenn Miller's single engine Norseman aircraft took off on 15th December 1944 and mysteriously disappeared somewhere over the Channel. A tragic end for a man whose music continues to have a special place in the memories of an entire generation on both sides of the Atlantic.

The Walk

From in front of the pub the walk crosses over the main road which it follows to the right on the road-side path. Over the end of Thurleigh Road it continues with the road for a short distance before turning left at a finger-post, up Church Green. Across the green can be seen All Saints Church, well worth a short diversion from the main route which turns right at the top of the green between two houses, one red brick, the other painted white. Past the garages behind the houses the path leads to a footbridge and stile over which it runs uphill, heading diagonally to the left across two small paddocks and a longer, rough pasture. At the top there are good views of the church and village below with Milton Ernest Hall set back from road. Through a metal gate the walk turns right and follows the hedgerow which eventually runs down to a cluster of large grain silos belonging to Mead Farm. From in front of the silos the existing right of way runs uphill again, across an arable field. At first the path sticks to the line of a hollow before bearing right to a good track along which it turns left. At the top of the rise it crosses the access road to Bedford Technology Park to another finger-post.

A good track continues ahead, but the existing right of way follows a path which at first angles left before dog-legging to the right down a very long, arable field. Eventually, it arrives at a cross tracks on the corner of what once was the perimeter track round Twinwoods Airfield.

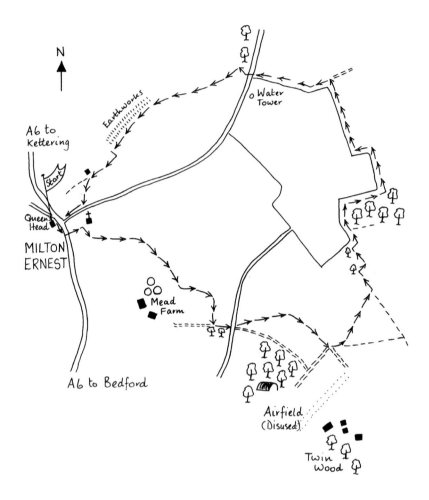

N

A6 to Kettering

Earthworks

Start

Queens Head

MILTON ERNEST

o Water Tower

Mead Farm

A6 to Bedford

Airfield (Disused)

Twin Wood

To the right, on the other side of the field, can be seen the old control tower in front of which the Glenn Miller Band gave an open-air concert to over a thousand American service personnel on the 27th August, 1944. A good stretch of the old perimeter track to the right is a public right of way and from this can be seen what remains of the buildings and open-ended blister hangers dotted round the edge of the field. The single runway, from which Glenn Miller's 'plane took-off on its ill-fated flight, used to run north to south in the middle of the field in front of the control tower. The modern Glenn Miller band played here as one of the events commemorating the fifty years since the 'D' Day landings and as a tribute to the memory of the man and his music.

From here the walk turns left along a good track, before turning left again where an oak post on the right indicates a path across another arable field. Through the hedge on the other side of this field, the path turns left and follows the hedge up the barbed-wire topped chain-link fence surrounding the site of Bedford Technology Park. At first the path is sandwiched between a wood and the fence but the going gets easier as the fence is followed left, away from the wood. After a few hundred yards a footbridge is crossed and the fence is again followed left up to an access road. Here the walk turns left, along the road for about fifty yards or so before bearing off to the right, still with the fence, up to a road.

In the distance to the right on this last stretch can be seen the hangars of Thurleigh Airfield from which the USAAF 306th Bomb Group flew four squadrons of B17s on daylight bombing raids over occupied Europe and the Third Reich. Chosen by Glenn Miller as the venue for the band's first major base concert, given in July 1944, over three thousand American airmen stood and cheered as the band played its opening number, *Moonlight Serenade*.

The walk crosses the road to an open gate on the left through which it follows the edge of a crop to the right. Within a few yards, it turns left on a path across the crop heading for the end of a hedge. Good views extend from right to left across the valley below as the walk reaches the hedge which is followed to the corner of the field. Over a footbridge the walk runs downhill, keeping to the left of a wide and fairly deep ditch of ancient appearance and speculative origins. Over another stile the route turns sharply left, along the hedge as far as a farm gate where it turns right, down the centre of the meadow to meet a drive to a house on the outskirts of Milton Ernest. Here the walk turns left and the drive is followed to Thurleigh Road along which it turns right, past the church and back down to the Queen's Head.

⑦ Tempsford
The Wheatsheaf

Tempsford is sited on what was the old Great North Road, the M1 of its era. The Wheatsheaf was built in 1799 as a staging post, just off the busy trunk road, in an attractive part of the village, known as Church End. As with most of the old coaching inns, it was originally built complete with stables and brew-house. Over the years these buildings have been incorporated to provide additional accommodation and, as a result, the interior retains its old world charm and cosy bar areas without being cramped. Outside, to the rear of the pub, is a large garden and children's play area.

A comprehensive menu provides a wide choice of home-cooked meals in the separate, 30-cover dining room, plus a good choice of bar meals. 'The Wheatsheaf Griddle' specialises in beef, lamb and gammon steaks, whilst a range of home-made pies and curries keep the regulars coming back for more. Bar snacks are available all day, every day. Traditional Sunday lunches are very popular, so booking in advance is advisable. The restaurant does not serve meals on Sunday nights. The Wheatsheaf is a Charles Wells pub and serves their Eagle IPA, Adnams Broadside plus a guest beer. Guinness,

Murphys, lager and cider are also available on draught. The landlord is a keen bridge and golf player who enjoys meeting fellow enthusiasts!

The opening times are Monday to Saturday from 11 am to 11 pm, and Sunday from noon to 10.30 pm.

Telephone: (01767) 640500.

How to get there: Tempsford is about 2 miles north of Sandy on the A1(T) road to St Neots. A slip road leads to Church End, where the pub stands opposite the church.

Parking: There is a car park behind the pub.

Length of the walk: 3½ miles. OS map Landranger 153 Bedford, Huntingdon; Explorer 208 Bedford and St Neots (GR 163531).

A relaxing walk along the banks of the River Ivel as far as the attractive village of Blunham. This delightful ramble now follows the final stretch of The Kingfisher Way, a route waymarked along the course of the river from Baldock to Tempsford (21 miles) as part of the Ivel Valley Countryside Project.

The Walk

From the pub the route goes through the churchyard of St Peter's opposite. After keeping to the right of the main door, it leaves the churchyard and turns left, down Mill Lane. Past a substantial converted barn is an immaculate, black and white, thatched cottage, which stands in front of the field where earthworks mark the site of the 12th century Gannocks Castle. The route continues past the mill and the lane becomes a track to the left of a cut. Eventually, a stile next to a gate is reached, over which the route turns left, away from the river. The path runs around two meadows before bearing right, over a small footbridge and stream and across to a large footbridge over the river Ivel.

The route crosses the river via the wooden bridge and turns left along the bank. A slightly raised path follows the river for a short distance and, after running under the overhead electricity cables, it turns right, on a headland path away from the river. The path eventually runs to the left of a large packing shed for locally grown vegetables, past which it becomes a track leading to a small lane. Here the route turns left and, after a good distance along the lane, meets the top of Blunham High Street on the outskirts of the village.

The route continues ahead down the High Street which, like most

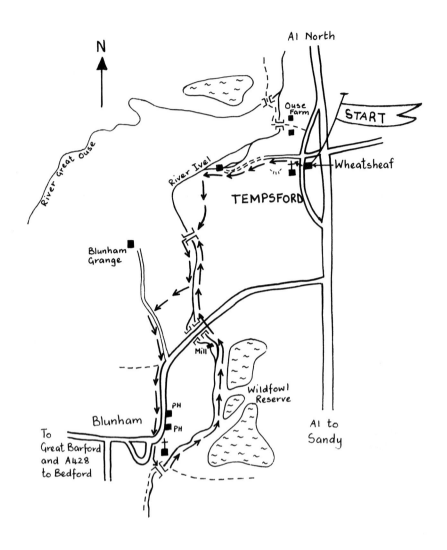

N

AI North

Ouse Farm

START

River Great Ouse

River Ivel

Wheatsheaf

TEMPSFORD

Blunham Grange

Mill

Wildfowl Reserve

PH

Blunham

PH

To
Great Barford
and A428
to Bedford

AI to
Sandy

others, gets more interesting the closer it gets to the centre of the village. Here the oldest houses cluster round the village church. Just before the road bends to the right, the Salutation Inn is passed on the left, closely followed by a second pub, the Horseshoes, on the corner where the road bends right. Round the corner the walk crosses over the road and turns down Park Lane, past the church of St James or St Edmund and the Old Rectory. Where Park Lane ends, the route turns left, down a broad, grassy track which leads to a footbridge and weir across the river. Over the footbridge the route turns left, via a stile, to follow the bank of the river downstream. This is a particularly attractive stretch of the river and the path first passes to the left of old gravel pit workings, now a large lake in private ownership, managed as a wildfowl reserve.

Further along the riverside path, the view of the lake is unfortunately concealed by a high bank. However, this is compensated for by arriving opposite where the river is divided round what is in effect an island, on which is sited an old mill.

Past the mill the path meets the road and crosses over, to the right of the new bridge, which extends the old five-arched bridge. From here the raised path continues along the river as it follows a fairly straight course across more open country. The walking is easy and relaxing, with only the occasional stile to break the pleasurable rhythm of putting one foot in front of the other. A willow tree or two is passed and, on a lucky day, herons may be seen close to the river. All too soon the opposite bank is recognised as having been walked on the outward leg and, shortly afterwards, the footbridge crossed earlier is reached.

Footpaths along either side of the riverbank above here are on private land and access is restricted to angling clubs. From here, therefore, the route turns right, away from the river and along the path used earlier which eventually leads back up Mill Lane to the pub.

On arriving in front of the Wheatsheaf, it is worth extending this walk if time permits, to the nearby confluence of the river Ivel and Bedfordshire's main river, the Great Ouse. Turn left from Mill Lane and follow the road for 100 yards or so to where a fingerpost indicates a path running down the drive to Ouse Farm. Past the end of the farmhouse it turns left, then right, through the middle of the farmyard – an experience in itself at milking time when the cows are encouraged to increase their milk yield by being serenaded with soothing music. Out the back of the farmyard a footbridge is crossed over the Ivel and the path turns right for the short distance up to where the river joins the Great Ouse. Swans and other waterfowl make themselves very much at home in the field adjoining the river. A finger of land can be walked to where the two rivers actually join. Alternatively, a more dramatic view can be enjoyed from the nearby bridge spanning the weir and river. The sight of this much water is very thirst making and a reminder, if one is needed, that it really is time to return to the pub.

8 Stevington
The Royal George

A limestone village, with a medieval market cross at its centre. To the east is the restored windmill and to the north-east the church, with its nearby spring which feeds a Holy Well. The pub was originally built as cottages and, following conversion to an inn, was named 'Royal George' after a famous sailing ship of the line, the flagship of Admiral Kemenfelt, which foundered and sank in Portsmouth harbour in 1782. Situated on Silver Street near the centre of the village, it is a small, homely, locals' pub, fast establishing a reputation for good, traditional pub food and well-kept beer.

A single bar serves the open-plan public and lounge areas and a modest, separate dining/families' room. Home-made main courses offer very good value for money and include popular beef and ale pies, whilst the Sunday lunch can be classed as a house speciality. Vegetarians are catered for and meals are served seven days a week. The Royal George is a free house currently serving Adnams Broadside and Wadworth 6X. There is a patio and garden area to the rear. Well-behaved dogs, kept on a lead, are allowed in the bars. The pub also holds the key for access to the windmill.

The opening times are Monday to Friday from noon to 2 pm and 5 pm to 11 pm and all day on Saturday and Sunday.
Telephone: (01234) 822184.

How to get there: Stevington is 3 miles north-west of Bedford and just north of the A428 midway between Turvey and Bromham. The Royal George is near the centre of the village, in Silver Street.

Parking: The pub fronts Silver Street, but the car park entrance is to the rear, from the Stevington to Pavenham road.

Length of the walk: 4½ miles (short cut available). OS map Landranger series 153 Bedford, Huntingdon and surrounding area; Explorer 208 Bedford and St Neots (GR 988532).

A walk with something for everyone, from an ancient church to a restored windmill; from lush, riverside meadows to high uplands. The second half includes a stretch of dismantled railway line, now a linear nature reserve designated the 'Stevington Country Walk'.
The whole village is well worth a stroll to better appreciate its many attractive houses and cottages. If time is limited, an enjoyable alternative to the circular walk would include a visit to the church and well, followed by a look at the windmill.

The Walk
From the pub the walk turns left, down Silver Street and keeps ahead over the crossroads in the centre of which stands a medieval market cross where John Bunyan is said to have preached. From here the walk joins the waymarked Bunyan Trail (see introduction) which at this point follows the lane ahead lined with attractive cottages. Church house with its community shop is passed on the left and is followed by much grander houses before St Marys church is reached at the end of the lane.
From here the walk bears right then left and follows the boundary wall of the churchyard into which is set a holy well fed from a nearby spring. Through a swing-gate the path continues ahead along the top of a bank with the river Great Ouse on the far side of the field to the right. Through an open gate it follows a hedge at the end of which it crosses to the other side of a barbed wire fence and continues ahead before turning left, along the edge of a wood. The path bears right with the wood and two stiles are crossed closely followed by another stile and footbridge. Here the walk turns left and leaves the Bunyan Trail (which continues ahead into Pavenham) as it turns left, heading for Westend on the outskirts of Stevington.
The path now runs slightly uphill following the line of the hedge

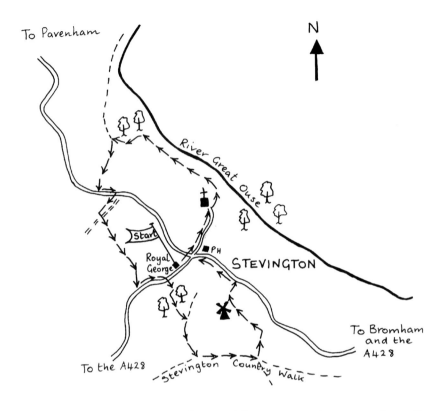

To Pavenham

N

River Great Ouse

Start

Royal
George

PH

STEVINGTON

To Bromham
and the
A428

To the A428

Stevington Country Walk

before bearing to the right of a metal farm-gate and over another stile from which a hedged path leads up to the road. At the road the route turns left, almost to the end of a row of terraced cottages where it crosses over to a roadside stile and fingerpost. From here a path is followed uphill again on a field edge path which is followed to another stile in the corner of the field. Over this it turns sharply left, crosses over a track and keeps ahead to where an oak post marks the line of the right of way on the brow of the hill. From this vantage point the windmill, the only surviving post-mill in the county, can be seen on the other side of the village below. The path now runs downhill with the hedge on the right and eventually meets the road where the route turns left, heading back into Stevington. (Those who want a shorter walk have the option of staying with the road back to The Royal George -see sketch map)

Opposite the first telephone pole on the left, the second half of the walk leaves the road as it turns right, on a footpath between garages. Over a stile it bears right, round the end of a garden before turning left over a stile and footbridge. From here a field edge path is followed ahead to a footbridge, over which the route turns right at a T-junction. The path now leads through bushes and trees before another footbridge is crossed to the old railway embankment, at the top of which, the route turns left.

Steam trains on branch lines such as this once provided a vital link for rural communities in the days when only the well-off could afford motor cars. They are still sorely missed by those old enough to recall the sight, sound and smell of them. Older members of the community still remember the day during the last war when all the women and children of the village turned out and ran across the fields to wave goodbye to the train carrying their men off to re-join the Beds and Herts regiment. With embarkation leave over they crammed the carriage windows cheering and waving on the first stage of a long journey that ended in Japanese slave-labour camps building the infamous 'railway of death', the Burma Railway.

Many of them didn't come back . . .

Today the embankment provides a valuable wildlife habitat and this stretch is part of the Stevington Country Walk. After a few hundred yards a wooden bench provides an ideal resting place from which to enjoy the view of the windmill. Further on the walk leaves the embankment as it turns left, in company with the Bunyan Trail once more. The walk stays with the track for a short distance before turning left, on a path which eventually leads to farm buildings. At this point a path to the left leads to the nearby postmill – so called because the body of the mill can be turned to face the direction of the wind. Dating from about 1770 the mill continued in operation until 1936, since when it has been restored several times.

Here the walk turns right on a track which soon reaches a road, along which the route turns left. Past the old chapel which now serves as a workshop for an organ builder, the road is followed back up to the crossroads and the pub.

9 Turvey
Ye Three Fyshes

Turvey is a 19th century, limestone, estate village. The river Great Ouse, on the western edge of the village, forms the border between Bedfordshire and Buckinghamshire. Below the ancient bridge across the river stand two statues, one nicknamed Jonah, and the other a female body with a male head, set up in 1953. Next to the bridge, flanked by a large mill sympathetically converted to private housing, is Ye Three Fyshes, a unique pub in an enviable setting. An inn has stood here for many centuries and probably derives its name from medieval times when it was largely believed that fish were the first living thing created by God, and were incorporated on coats of arms.

Informality is the key to the pub's rambling interior which includes a large, comfortable bar with open fire, plus smoking and non-smoking dining areas. There is a wide selection of home-cooked food from the more exotic, such as gleftiko lamb, to traditional favourites such as beefsteak and ale pie. Daily deliveries of high quality, fresh fish means that fish dishes are a house speciality. There is a choice of three or four roast dinners on a Sunday, plus the normal menu. Vegetarians are always catered for and meals are served throughout the week. Ye Three Fyshes is a Greene King pub serving their IPA, Ruddles County plus a guest beer. Guinness, lager and cider are also available, and an extensive wine list complements the wide choice of home cooked food. There is a very pleasant riverside garden to the rear of the pub.

The opening times are Monday to Friday 11 am to 3 pm and 6 pm to 11 pm, Saturday 11 am to 11 pm and on Sunday from noon to 10.30 pm. Telephone: (01234) 881264.

How to get there: Turvey is 6 miles west of Bedford, on the A428 Bedford to Northampton road. Ye Three Fyshes is on the main road, on the western side of the village, next to the bridge.

Parking: There is a car park on the same side of the road as the pub, but about 100 yards away from it towards the centre of the village.

Length of the walk: 5 miles. OS map Landranger series 153 Bedford, Huntingdon and surrounding area; Explorer 208 Bedford and St Neots (GR 939524).

This walk links the two villages of Turvey and Carlton. From the centre of Turvey with its attractive limestone cottages and church, the route travels northwards, across rising ground and arable farmland. From St Mary's church on the outskirts of Carlton, it follows the road almost into the village before turning south on bridle tracks with fine views over the valley to the north. The last stage of the walk includes Abbey Park, created in the 17th century, and passes Turvey Abbey, originally built as a farm but now used by a Benedictine order of monks and nuns.

The Walk

From the pub the route turns right, along the roadside path. At the crossroads it turns left, up past the Three Cranes inn, followed by the lodge and entrance to Turvey House in front of All Saints church, one of the finest and oldest churches in the diocese of St Albans. At the post office the route turns left, up Carlton Road and then right, opposite Chantry Farm, along May Road. After 50 yards or so it turns left, along Grove Road, at the end of which a swing-gate gives access to playing fields.

On the other side of the playing fields, another swing-gate leads to a path which continues ahead across arable fields, past the end of a line of trees. From here it continues in the same direction across more fields, then across a footbridge over a deep ditch. It crosses a track and continues running slightly uphill to the corner of a field, from where it bears right, heading for a stile in the opposite corner. Over a track followed by a double stile and footbridge, it runs diagonally right, across a pasture. Over another stile the path continues in the same

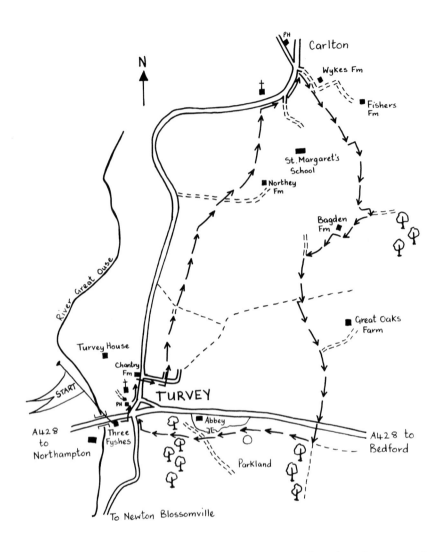

direction, then over a wire fence and stile each side of a second pasture. From here it crosses a final, arable field, aiming for the church tower, to a roadside stile in the corner.

In front of St Mary's church, with its splendid weathercock, the route turns right along the roadside path. Past the entrance to St Margaret's Boarding School on the right, and just before the village sign for Carlton is reached, the route turns right, along a metalled farm road leading to three farms.

Before turning right, there is an opportunity to carry on ahead to the village of Carlton, which has two pubs. For those who may be in need of urgent refreshment at this halfway stage, the Fox is closer to hand, about 100 yards down the left-hand turn from the T-junction, just past the village sign.

After leaving the road, the metalled track runs past a barn and where it turns left, the route carries straight on ahead, through a gateway and along a bridleway track. From here it continues across pasture up to a hedge, along which it turns left. Through another gate it turns right, on a track running up and over the top of a rise. From here, there are wide views across the countryside to the north before the track runs downhill, keeping to the left of the hedge. At the bottom of the hill it follows a stream on the right for a short distance, before continuing round the field on a headland path. Where the hedge on the right ends, it turns right, and right again to follow a wide, grassy track. Soon the track turns right, past the old barns of Bagden Farm, after which it turns left, and follows the hedgeline to a cross-tracks. Here it turns left again, through an open gateway, and along a track running across arable fields. In the corner of the field the path dog-legs right, then left, through a swing gate. From here it continues ahead down the side of a wide sheep pasture before meeting the farm road to Great Oaks Farm. Over a cattle-grid the route stays with the farm road over a rise and down to the main road, which it crosses straight over. A track now runs ahead for 100 yards or so before crossing a footbridge, where the route turns right, over a stile, to enter Abbey Park.

The park was created in the 17th century and fine specimens of oak, large-leaved lime and field maple survive within its boundaries. The path first keeps to the left of a fallen tree. From here it continues ahead, across pasture, to a stile in the opposite fence. It then keeps to the right of the 'Royal Anniversary Roundel' of trees planted to commemorate the Queen's 40th year on the throne. Past the roundel, it bears to the right to follow the left-hand bank of a stream. Over another stile next to a gate, Turvey Abbey can be seen on the right, set in its own grounds on the edge of the park. Originally, Turvey Abbey was built as a farm and, in spite of its name, was not monastic. However, since 1980 it has served a purpose more in keeping with its name as it was then purchased by a Roman Catholic Order of Benedictine monks and nuns.

The path bears left, across a track into the park, after which it goes over a stile and follows a path through a belt of woodland. Two long paddocks and three stiles eventually lead to a track which continues ahead down to the road. Here the route turns right, back down to the crossroads in the centre of the village, where a final, left-hand, turn leads back to the pub.

Everton
The Thornton Arms

Everton is a ridge-top village with a church and some attractive, thatched cottages. The name of the pub is connected to the local landed gentry, whilst the pub itself was purpose built in 1852. Originally, it was part of a 72-acre homestead, complete with coach-house and its own brew-house. Today, it is a friendly village pub, popular with the locals and with walkers. Separate bars serve two open-plan areas, one of which is graced by an original, rainbow coloured Rockola American juke box. There is a separate dining room serving a range of home-cooked meals including chilli con carne and chicken tikka masala as house specialities. Meals are not available on Sundays, although snacks are available by prior arrangement.

The Thornton Arms is a freehouse with a reputation for well-kept beer. On offer is Charles Wells Eagle IPA and two guest beers, for example, Bombardier and Wadworth 6X. Fargo Velvet, cider and lager are also available on draught. There is a pleasant garden area to the rear of the pub. Dogs are not allowed inside, as three are already in residence.

The opening times are Monday to Friday from noon to 3 pm and 6 pm to 11 pm, Saturday from noon to 11 pm, and Sunday from noon to 10.30 pm.

Telephone: (01767) 681149.

How to get there: Everton is located just over 1 mile north-east of Sandy. Turn off the B1042 Sandy to Potton road near the station. The pub is on the main road at the centre of the village, by the cul-de-sac leading to the church.

Parking: There is a car park behind the pub. If it is full, use the waste ground area in front of the church.

Length of the walk: 4 miles. OS map Landranger series 153 Bedford, Huntingdon and surrounding area; Explorer 208 Bedford and St Neots (GR 203513).

This walk begins by following a gated estate road along the line of the ridge, with fine views. Having descended the ridge to the flat plain below, the return leg incorporates a visit to one of Bedfordshire's best kept secrets of World War II.

The Walk

From the pub, the route turns right, down the cul-de-sac leading to Church End and along the Greensand Ridge Walk (GRW). Past the church of St Mary on the right the route follows the gated estate road along the line of the ridge. Arable fields on either side of the road are soon replaced by parkland used as sheep grazing. Storey Farm is passed on the left, a fine example of a 19th century farm, with substantial barns surrounding a traditional yard. The farmhouse itself is a delightful Victorian, tile faced building, with a plaque displaying the family arms and the date, 1884.

The route continues along the estate road, through attractive parkland planted with a mixture of broadleaved trees and the occasional clump of Scots pine. At a crossroads it continues ahead, with Woodbury Hall to the left. Where the road eventually bends left, the route continues ahead over the grass and through a white metal swing-gate. From here it crosses an arable field to a stile, where the route leaves the GRW (which turns right), as it turns left, along a track.

The route now follows the waymarked circular walk past white gates on the left leading to Woodbury Home Farm. The path descends from the ridge quite steeply before bearing left, along the edge of a wood. Be prepared for muddy feet on this stretch, especially after wet weather. The route then turns right along a concrete track which provides much better going as it angles its way left and right round large, arable fields on the flat plain at the base of the ridge. Past a small

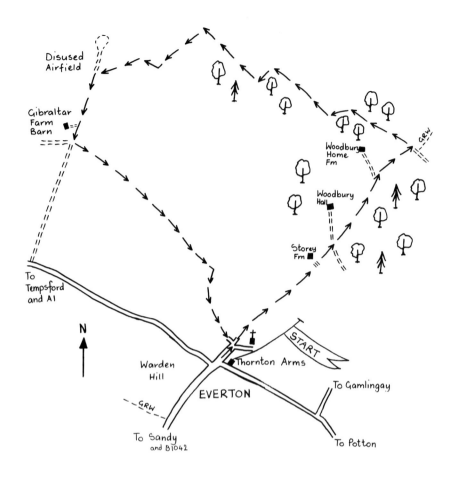

wood, Everton church can be seen on top of the ridge, behind which
the Sandy TV transmitter mast serves as a handy landmark.

Eventually, a track is reached running along the line of the old
Roman road, which went from Sandy to Godmanchester. Here the
route turns left along this ancient way, which in more recent times
served as the perimeter track for RAF Tempsford during World War
II. After a short distance, turn right, off the track, to visit the small,
very ordinary looking barn, which played an extraordinary part in the
war against Germany at a time when the Third Reich stretched as far
as the English Channel.

During the war, RAF Tempsford was a secret base for the SOE
(Special Operations Executive). From here, 161 and 138 Squadrons,
flying Halifaxes and Lysanders, dropped or landed over 1,000 agents

in enemy occupied Europe. Many agents and aircrew failed to return from their hazardous missions and this barn, where they.kitted up before taking off, is maintained as a humble memorial to their sacrifice on our behalf. Inside the barn are touching tributes and messages left by those who have made the pilgrimage to this special place, whilst, outside, newly planted trees are dedicated to the memory of individual agents, such as the first American serviceman killed on an SOE 'Carpetbagger' operation. Another is to those who died fighting for the freedom of Norway as members of the Norwegian Resistance Movement. Amongst the many tributes to these brave men and women is one from the Bedford Ramblers and the Long Distance Walkers – 'Lest we Forget'.

Back on the ex-perimeter track, what is left of the old main runway is now used as a general storage area, whilst across the other side of the field can be seen a surviving hangar. From here the route turns left, off the perimeter track, to follow the circular walk along a raised track. After a good distance the track bears right before climbing back up the ridge to emerge at the top, next to a pair of small, thatched cottages. From here a lane leads from the outskirts of Everton to a T-junction, where it turns right along the road walked earlier, back to the pub.

⑪ Bedford
The George and Dragon

Bedford is the county's principal administrative centre and market town, with a long history dating back to the 10th century as an important trading place. Historically, it has always been important as a meeting of ways across the river Great Ouse, and was recorded in AD 880 as 'Bedanford', meaning 'Beda's ford'. Today, in addition to its thriving market, it has developed as an excellent shopping centre whilst still retaining much of its charm, especially in the riverside areas and some of its old hostelries.

The George and Dragon is a fine example of a late 18th century coaching inn, complete with an arch to the rear leading to a yard and stables. A handsome and substantial red-brick building, it is situated almost at the centre of the town, just off the High Street and takes pride in its reputation as a busy, up-market pub. Inside, the pub has a spacious lounge bar with a very pleasant conservatory extension. Upstairs, there is a function room which in its time has seen service as a boxing gym, a snooker hall, and, during the 1960s, a venue for well-known traditional jazz bands. Downstairs again, there is a no-smoking dining room in addition to the conservatory dining area. There is a choice of over forty bar-snacks, such as toasted steak and salad sandwiches, to full à la carte meals beginning with home made soups and supplemented by The George and Dragon's renowned cheeseboard. Meals are available throughout the week, including Sundays when there is a choice of traditional roasts. There is a courtyard area behind the conservatory for use in fine weather. This is a Greene King pub serving IPA and Abbot Ale from the cask. Draught Guinness, two ciders and six lagers are also available.

The opening times are Monday to Saturday, all day from 11 am to 11 pm and on Sunday from noon to 11 pm.

Telephone: (01234) 345061.

How to get there: Bedford is on the A6 between Luton and Rushden, midway between the M1 (junctions 13 and 14), and the A1(T), taking either the A428 or A603 from the latter. The pub is in the centre of Bedford. Turn off the High Street at the traffic lights, down Mill Street.

Parking: There is a small car park to the rear of the pub, opposite which is a large public car park with plenty of room.

Length of the walk: 4 miles. OS map Landranger 153, Bedford, Huntingdon; Explorer 208 Bedford and St Neots (GR 052498).

A walk full of interest and all the more remarkable for the fact that within a relatively short distance from busy Bedford, peace and quiet reign in a tranquil, lakeside setting. This walk also has the advantage of being accessible to wheelchairs and pushchairs for much of its length.

The Walk
From the George and Dragon, the route turns right along Mill Street. Within a short distance the Bunyan Meeting House and adjacent museum is passed, the first, but not the last, reminder of the county's most famous writer.

John Bunyan was born in Bedfordshire and plaques in the town commemorate his life, from his birthplace in Harrowden, to the site of the nearby jail where he was incarcerated for twelve years. Unbroken in spirit, with a prison cell as his 'hermitage' , he proved once more the truth of the poem by Lovelace that 'Stone walls do not a prison make', by writing his allegorical masterpiece, *The Pilgrim's Progress*. The museum covers his life and works and the Meeting House, in addition to its fine bronze doors, has five stained glass windows depicting Pilgrim and his Progress.

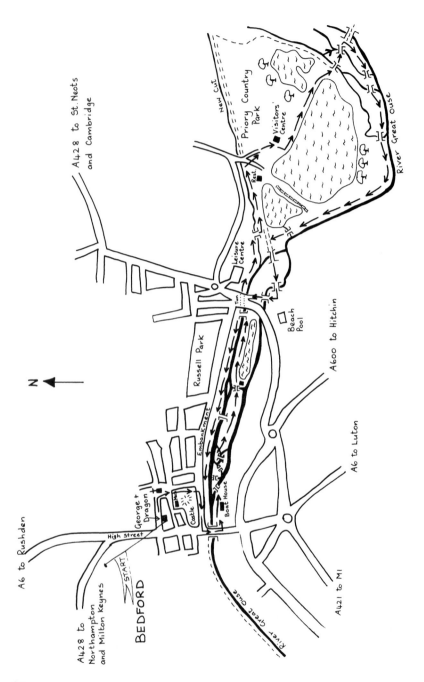

Past the Meeting House the route turns right, along Newnham Road, with the Polish community's Roman Catholic church of St Cuthbert on the opposite side. It then crosses over Castle Road to enter, via an ornamental ironwork gate, the castle grounds and the gardens surrounding the Bedford Museum and the Cecil Higgins Art Gallery.

The gallery's collection is of national importance and includes ceramics and glass as well as works by famous artists such as Gainsborough, Constable, Cotman and Turner. Bedford Museum is housed in a converted brewery and has comprehensive displays relating to the county's geology, archaeology, natural history and social history. It is open on Tuesday to Saturday from 11 am to 5 pm and Sunday and bank holidays from 2 pm to 5 pm. Telephone: (0234) 353323.

From the entrance the route follows the path ahead to the left of the castle mound, all that remains of a castle built on this site shortly after the Norman Conquest. After passing through a small garden, the path meets the road along the embankment of the river Great Ouse, which flows through the centre of the town. This side of the river is paved for some distance and the attractive Embankment Gardens provide shady seats from which to observe river activity. The town has a distinguished rowing history and club boathouses line the river bank. Apart from rowing activity, this very pleasant stretch of the river, with its conveniently placed seats, provides a chance to feed and observe the numerous ducks, geese and swans.

Having crossed over the road, the route turns right, past the Swan Hotel and along the embankment up to the T-junction with the main road. Here it turns left to cross over the five-arched Town Bridge, built in the early 1800s. On the other side of the river, the route turns left, down to the river bank, and past the front of the Bedford Rowing Club boathouse. The path then follows the right-hand river bank over several small, wooden bridges before turning left, over Weir Bridge.

The path continues past the spot where Bunyan was baptised in the river, whilst to the right, across King's Ditch, stand the town houses of Duckmill Crescent as proof that modern development can be sympathetic to its surroundings. Further along the path, the lock, which provides access to navigable waters from here to the Wash at King's Lynn, is crossed. Past the bandstand the route continues ahead.

The suspension bridge on the left provides a convenient short-cut at this point for those who are pressed for time or who prefer a short stroll.

After crossing Mill Weir Bridge, the path runs past the front of another boathouse, with Longholme boating lake on the right (rowing boats for hire, light refreshments and ice-cream); From here it continues to follow the river bank over Mill Meadows, until it turns left over a pedestrian bridge just before the road.

Over the bridge the route turns right, down through the subway under the main road to emerge on the river bank next to the Aspects leisure park. The path continues ahead, along the riverbank, past a small weir, and then bears left round a car park before turning right, across a bridge. Over the bridge, it turns left, along a good track which is, in fact, a dismantled railway line, now designated the Bedford to Willington Country Way. Further on, the route leaves the track as it turns right through the main entrance to Priory Country Park. On the far side of the car park ahead is a visitors' centre, open throughout the year (not on Saturdays).

The centre contains full information and interpretive displays. Bedford Borough Council manages the park, created from old gravel workings and extending to 228 acres, including 80 acres of water. In addition to water sports and fishing, the park contains special wildlife conservation zones. Footpaths can be followed round these areas and seasonal trail leaflets can be obtained from the visitors' centre which provide a useful and informative basis on which the main route can be extended.

Past the visitors' centre, the route turns left to follow a metalled path around the lake's perimeter. At the bottom of the lake the route turns left, over a wooden bridge, to the right of which the canoe slalom can be seen. A second bridge takes the path to Cardington Lock, which marks the end of surfaced paths and therefore, the limit of the walk for the easy handling of wheelchairs and pushchairs. (It would be advisable for those with wheelchairs and pushchairs to retrace the route rather than go beyond this point as the river bank path is often muddy and soft going.) Just before reaching the lock, the route turns right on a stony track along the river bank. After several riverside bridges, the path passes the end of an ancient wall, once part of the priory from which the Country Park gets its name. Past the wall, the path continues along the river bank before going over a bridge behind the marina. After the bridge the path forks right, away from the river, as it crosses a rough pasture before climbing the bank back onto the line of the dismantled railway. Here the route turns left and, after crossing two iron bridges over the river, continues ahead to a meeting of the ways next to the dramatic, pyramidal shape of Bedford's 'Oasis'.

The route turns right to cross a pedestrian bridge over the river, on the other side of which it turns left, under the road. From here there is a choice of walking either side of the river before retracing the outward route back to the pub.

12 Wrestlingworth
The Chequers

Wrestlingworth is a pleasant village, with the Chequers close to the crossroads at its centre. Built prior to 1727, when it was known as the Three Horseshoes, it has been much altered and extended over the years and now incorporates what was once the village smithy. Inside, wooden beams and the original open fireplaces make the age of the building more apparent. An additional claim to fame locally is that on one occasion in the past it served as a temporary mortuary in which a post-mortem on the body of a local murder victim was conducted! Today, however, there is no hint of its ghoulish past to be found in the bright and cheerful interior.

A single long bar serves open-plan, comfortable and roomy areas decorated with an impressive collection of horse brasses. The accommodation is spacious enough to allow for a separate dining area and a good selection of home-made main courses is available. In addition there is a wide variety of bar snacks. A friendly, welcoming pub, popular as a 'local', with a good passing trade. The Chequers is a Greene King pub and serves their Abbot Ale, IPA and XX Mild. A guest ale, Guinness, cider and lager are also available on draught. Outside there is a small patio, plus a garden and children's play area.

The opening times are Monday to Thursday from noon to 2 pm and 6 pm to 11 pm. Friday and Saturday from noon to 3 pm and 6 pm to 11 pm, and on Sunday from noon to 3 pm and 7 pm to 10.30 pm. The pub is closed Monday·lunchtimes.

Telephone: (01767) 631256.

How to get there: Wrestlingworth is situated just inside the Bedfordshire/Cambridgeshire border, 5 miles east of Sandy. From the A1(T), take either the B1042 at Sandy, or the B1040 at Biggleswade. The pub is at the centre of the village, on the B1042 (High Street).

Parking: There is a large car park to one side of the pub.

Length of the walk: 3½ miles. OS map Landranger series 153 Bedford, Huntingdon and surrounding area; Explorer 208 Bedford and St Neots (GR 257475).

A walk, which includes a short stretch of the Clopton Way, over vast, upland prairies, with views across rolling farmland into Cambridgeshire. A memorial in the churchyard at Cockayne Hatley reveals something guaranteed to bring an instant smile of recognition to everyone's face. How many memorials of more elaborate design in more grandiose surroundings could claim as much?

The Walk

From the pub the route turns left, along the roadside path, past the village post office. At the T-junction it continues ahead and forks left along Butcher's Lane. In front of the last house it negotiates a fence on the left. Over the fence it turns right across a pasture behind houses, to a stile next to a gate in the opposite corner. From here it keeps ahead across the bottom end of a garden before turning left, along a headland path skirting an arable field. Over a ditch it turns right, along a narrow, concrete track. At a ditch, the route turns right and keeps ahead across the field before passing through a belt of trees. On the other side of the trees it turns left on a track leading up to the road, where it turns right, along the grass verge.

At the top of the long rise it turns right, along a bridleway track which runs in a northerly direction towards the distant water-tower. There are good all-round views from here, with the farming uplands of Cambridgeshire to the east and Sandy TV mast behind Potton below in the valley to the west.

The route follows the track ahead, over a cross-tracks, and

54

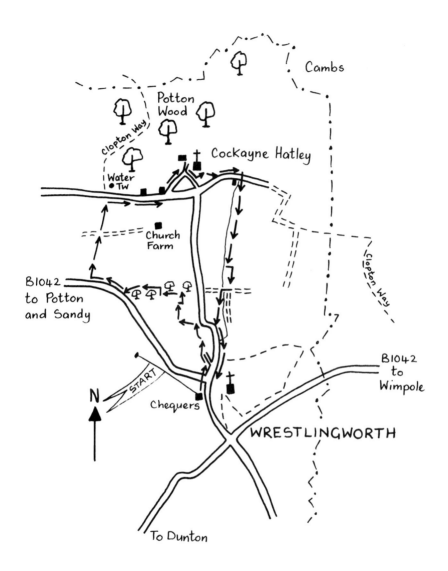

Cambs

Potton Wood

Clopton Way

Water Tw

Cockayne Hatley

Clopton Way

Church Farm

B1042 to Potton and Sandy

B1042 to Wimpole

WRESTLINGWORTH

N

START

Chequers

To Dunton

eventually turns right, along a lane in front of the water-tower. The route now coincides with the Clopton Way. Some distance along the lane it turns left down the right-hand side of the second house on the left, along a drive down to the church. At a junction and waymarked oak post in front of the church, the walk turns right. At the end of the churchyard it turns left, on a field-path.

Through the imposing, brick built gateway to Cockayne Hatley Hall is the church of St John the Baptist which has a unique collection of baroque woodwork from Belgium, while the churchyard has a convenient seat from which to admire the memorial referred to earlier.

The memorial is to W.E. Henley, Victorian journalist and minor poet. The enduring claim to fame of this larger than life one-legged character is his association with many of the more famous men of letters of his time. As a friend of R.L. Stevenson, Henley is thought to have served as inspiration for one the most famous characters in children's literature – Long John Silver! His daughter referred to J.M. Barrie, also known to the family, as her 'fwendy' – hence 'Wendy' in *Peter Pan*.

Past the bottom of the churchyard, the path continues in the same direction across a small arable field, on the other side of which it meets the lane into the hamlet of Cockayne Hatley. On the right-hand side the lane first runs past Well House, with its unusual pump, then the Old Rectory. Further along, abandoned sheds on the other side of the lane were once used as a packing station in the days when this area supported a vast acreage of apple orchards. Opposite the sheds, the route turns right, on a footpath down the left-hand side of a house.

Clear of the hedge and garden, the headland path follows a stream along the line of which a single row of seedling trees makes a poor substitute for the lost orchards. After the first huge, arable field, the path turns left, away from the stream, then right, following the line of a hedge and ditch. Where it meets a track the route turns right for a few yards, continuing past a T-junction after which it turns left, along the right-hand bank of the stream again. At the end of the small field the path is fenced-in as it continues ahead along the side of a pasture. It then runs between the houses on the outskirts of Wrestlingworth.

Just past the houses, the track meets the road which the route follows through the village. Eventually, the outward route is rejoined at Butcher's Lane, and from here it is followed back to the pub.

13 Old Warden
The Hare and Hounds

Old Warden is an estate village, mainly created by the third Lord Ongley in the 19th century. The Victorian, 'Swiss chocolate box' style of the thatched cottages, together with the Swiss Garden adjoining the Shuttleworth Collection of antique but airworthy aircraft, make the village popular with tourists during the summer months. As a result, the Hare and Hounds can be very busy during this season.

Originally converted from cottages, the building has seen a number of changes over the years. Four bars, in which food is served, are pleasantly and comfortably furnished. On offer is a wide range of home-cooking; traditional, international and vegetarian tastes are all catered for. The Hare and Hounds is a Charles Wells house currently serving Eagle IPA and Bombardier, plus a guest beer. Guinness and lager are also available on draught. There is a large and very pleasant garden to the rear of the pub plus a paved courtyard, ideal for al fresco party gatherings in the summer. Dogs are allowed inside the public bar.

The opening times are Tuesday to Saturday from noon to 3 pm and 6 pm to 11 pm, and on Sunday from noon to 10.30 pm. The pub is currently closed on Monday.

Telephone: (01767) 627225.

How to get there: Old Warden is about 4 miles south-east of Bedford and 2 miles west of Biggleswade. Turn off the A600 Bedford to Shefford road on the B658 and follow signs for Swiss Garden and the Shuttleworth Collection. Alternatively, take the B658 off the A1(T) at Sandy. The Hare and Hounds is on the only road through the village, next to the village post office.

Parking: There is a large car park to one side of the pub. Additional parking is available at the village hall.

Length of the walk: 4 miles (or shorter option). OS map Landranger series 153 Bedford, Huntingdon and surrounding area; Explorer 208 Bedford and St Neots (GR 138439).

An excellent walk, over fields and through trees, at any time of the year, including a chance to see one of the most unusual church interiors in the county. In spring, the daffodils throughout the village and the bluebells in the woods make this delightful circuit extra-special.

The Walk

From the pub the route turns left along the road. Just past the next-door village post office, on the opposite side of the road, is a waymarked path which the route follows down the side of a thatched cottage. At the end of the field, wooden steps climb a steep bank, at the top of which the path bears right, and then left in the corner of the field. Ignore the metal swing-gate ahead, which is used on the return journey.

From here the headland path follows the hedge along the edge of two fields. At a T-junction, the route turns right on a narrow track, before turning left where a wooden swing-gate on the right leads to the nearby church. (You could take the path to the church and then return to the pub, if time permits only a short pre/post prandial stroll.)

Having turned left, the route continues along the track and carries on ahead over a cross-tracks as it enters Palmers Wood, which contains areas of ancient woodland and is carpeted with primroses and bluebells in the spring. Other wildlife likely to be seen or heard are woodpeckers, and muntjac deer.

The track runs through a grassy clearing in the middle of the wood, with a white wooden hut on the left, from where it continues for some distance before coming to the end of the trees. Here it turns right, and

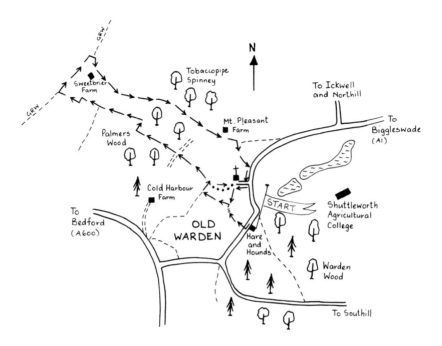

then left, on a headland path running round the edge of two large arable fields. The path continues ahead, ignoring fingerposts at the end of the first field. At a corner it crosses a footbridge as it dog-legs left, then right and follows the hedge up to a T-junction. Here, the route turns right, along the Greensand Ridge Walk (GRW).

There are good views to the north-west along the line of the ridge and, looming over the landscape in the distance, are the twin hulks of the Cardington airship sheds. The largest of their kind to survive in Europe, big enough to house 1,000 dinosaurs, they were once home to the ill-fated R101 and her sister ship the R102. Following the loss of the R101, which crashed on its maiden voyage on a hillside in France, the R102 was broken up for scrap and the airship era came to an abrupt end.

The route follows the track along the ridge, past the remnants of a hedge and then an occasional ash tree (look for the very dead but still standing tree that was struck by lightning). The path turns right at a waymarked oak post and, after a short distance, crosses a footbridge over a ditch and leaves the GRW, turning right, along a sandy track. Soon the farmhouse of Sweetbrier Farm is passed on the right. A substantial 17th century timber-framed house, it was refronted in the 18th century and was once known as Standalone Farm, due to its isolated position.

Past the farm, the route continues to follow the stony track across more arable fields before going through the other end of Palmers Wood and Tobaccopipe Spinney. Clear of these woods, Mount Pleasant Farm is passed – the very epitome of a modern, agri-business farm, with barns the size of aircraft hangars dwarfing its original farmhouse. After the farm, the track becomes a concrete drive and, where it turns right, there is a good view of Shuttleworth Agricultural College, once the home of the Shuttleworth family.

Where the drive meets the road, the route turns right, past a row of almost doll-sized cottages with a water-pump complete with thatched roof on the opposite side of the road. At the end of the cottages, the route turns right, past a larger thatched cottage and up a narrow lane leading to the village church.

St Leonard's dates back to the early 12th century and whilst some may consider its interior over elaborate, it is, nevertheless, of exceptional interest. A guide book on sale in the church gives full details, but what impresses, if not overwhelms, the casual visitor is its masses of wood-carvings. On leaving the church, read the poignant inscription in the porch, built by Mrs Dorothy Shuttleworth as a memorial to her only son, 'the last squire of Old Warden' , killed in action whilst flying with the RAF in World War II.

From here the route leaves via a metal swing-gate opposite the church. A path follows the fence on the edge of a small pasture before going through another swing-gate where the outward route is rejoined. Go along this path, then left, back down the wooden steps, to return to the village and the pub.

Broom
(14) The Cock

Broom is unusual in having no church but two pubs. Of the latter, The Cock is unique in Bedfordshire in that it has no bar and still retains many of the characteristics of a Victorian ale house. It occupies a row of cottages in which the beer was originally served in just one room, the beer being directly drawn from casks in the cellar. Today, against all the odds, the tradition of serving direct from the cask survives and customers are waited upon in rooms that have not been altered to any large extent over the years and which still retain their original proportions and general appearance.

A quarry tiled public bar off the open cellar is comfortably furnished with settles and chairs and there is a larger, separate and very pleasant room for dining. In addition, there is a cosy wood-panelled snug complete with open fire, and two more similar rooms to the front, one with a collection of old bottles, the other a games room with dartboard and table skittles. There is a garden with children's play area to the rear of the pub. Well behaved dogs are welcome, but restricted to the public bar.

In keeping with its traditional image, the pub serves generous portions of excellent, home-cooked English 'pub-grub' – soups,

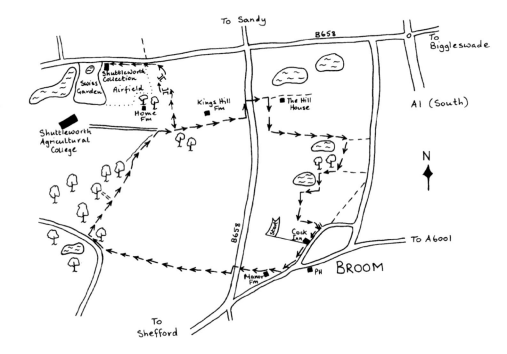

hotpot, and ploughman's lunches. Meals are available throughout the week, with the exception of Sunday evenings. The Cock is a Greene King pub and serves their IPA, Abbot and Ruddles County. Guinness, cider and two lagers are also available on draught. The opening times are Monday to Friday from noon to 3 pm and 6 pm to 11 pm, on Saturday from noon to 4 pm and 6 pm to 11 pm and on Sunday from noon to 4 pm and 7 pm to 10.30 pm.

Telephone: (01767) 314411.

How to get there: From the A6001 between Biggleswade and Shefford, take the B658. Turn off the B658 for the High Street on which the pub is located, close to the green.

Parking: There is a car park behind the pub.

Length of the walk: 5 miles (add an extra mile if visiting the Shuttleworth Collection and/or the Swiss Garden). OS map Landranger series 153 Bedford, Huntingdon and surrounding area; Explorer 208 Bedford and St Neots (GR 172430).

A walk across the prairie-like farmscape of mid-Bedfordshire plus a chance to visit the Shuttleworth Collection of airworthy vintage aircraft and/or the adjoining Swiss Garden. Also the Bird of Prey and Conservation Centre, telephone (01767) 627752.

The Walk

From the pub the route turns right, along the road and past the village green on the other side of which is The White Horse. Where the row of thatched houses on the right ends, it turns right off the road on a bridleway across the bottom end of a first, arable, field. Past the barns it keeps ahead on a drive down to the road which it dog-legs across left, then right, to continue on a track which runs unswervingly for a good ½ mile across huge arable fields.

To the left, ahead across the fields, can be seen the village of Southill, much of which was built by the Whitbread family. To the right is the occasional glimpse of the tower of what is now the Shuttleworth Agricultural College. What impresses most, however, is the giant scale of these fields from which the hedgerows and the associated wildlife have vanished and in which mainly skylarks and the occasional hare now survive.

The track eventually meets the road, down which the route carries on ahead for a short distance before turning right, on another bridleway track. Over the first, wide, field it continues ahead at a T-junction and along the edge of a newly planted wood. At the end of the field the route bears left, through an opening, to follow a stream across a further field, in the far corner of which it meets the main drive to Shuttleworth Agricultural College. Here the route turns right and follows the drive. After a bridge is crossed, those wishing to continue to the Shuttleworth Collection at Old Warden airfield and/or the Swiss Garden turn left, through a swing-gate.

Those who do not wish to make this visit, which adds a mile or so to the overall length of the walk, should keep ahead down the drive, following the direction given in the final paragraph.

Having turned left, off the drive through the swing-gate, the route crosses a small pasture, on the other side of which it goes through a field-gate. From here it passes a pond on the left and runs along the banks of a stream before turning left over a wide footbridge. The path then turns right to follow the other bank of the stream with the aircraft hangars of Old Warden in view to the left. The path turns right, over another footbridge, and then follows the stream to the road where the route turns left. A few hundred yards along the road, the main entrance to the airfield and the Shuttleworth Collection is reached, whilst just past the roadside hangar is the entrance to the adjoining Swiss Garden.

The Shuttleworth Collection is famous as the home of the largest private collection of airworthy vintage aircraft in the country. The hangars are contemporary with the aircraft they house and the overall effect is that of a classic, pre-war, grass landing-field from the era of *Those Magnificent Men in their Flying Machines*. Flying display days are held throughout the summer and a static exhibition of various types, both civil and military, is open throughout the year, except for up to two weeks over Christmas and New Year. Amenities include a small café/ restaurant and a gift-shop. Telephone: (01767) 627288.

The adjoining Swiss Garden is a time-warp of a different nature, described as 'a romantic garden in the heart of Bedfordshire'. Created in the ornate style fashionable in the 1820s, it has a 'Swiss' cottage on a rounded hill in its centre from which the garden gets its name. Paths lead across ornamental ironwork bridges to tiny islands and other delights such as the Fernery and Grotto, the brilliantly-coloured Indian Kiosk and the miniature chapel. The garden has a fine collection of trees and shrubs and is particularly attractive in the spring and early summer when the daffodils are succeeded by azaleas and rhododendrons. Open daily March to September, Sundays only January, February and October. For further information, telephone (01767) 627666.

Having visited the Shuttleworth Collection and.or the Swiss Garden, the route is retraced to the driveway to Shuttleworth College. Here, it turns left along the drive and, after passing the most attractive farmhouse and garden of King's Hill Farm, it continues to a busy main road. Here the route turns left along the roadside path. Past the houses on the left, the road is crossed to a bridleway track on the other side. This track crosses an area which will be restored following gravel extraction to provide new, landscaped lakes for the benefit of both leisure and wildlife. Across a temporary bridge over a conveyor belt, the walk turns right on a way-marked track. After a short distance the track turns left and is followed almost to the road just before which a footpath is followed to the right. Across a footbridge it keeps just inside a wood before turning right, still following the wood which it leaves as it turns left then right round a small, newly landscaped lake complete with islands. Leaving the lake it turns left and left again on a main track leading past houses to the road into Broom. Here the road is followed right, back to the pub.

⑮ Houghton Conquest
The Knife and Cleaver

The Knife and Cleaver stands opposite the church in the centre of the village. It is an up-market restaurant and hotel which has retained its pub origins, with a very pleasantly furnished lounge bar serving real ale, and there is an additional room for families with children.

A deservedly high reputation has been built up for the home-cooked food, which uses the best of local produce. The meals served, could be described as English food with a French flavour – including such dishes as smoked fish flan with a black olive and leek salad, pan fried lamb steaks marinaded in Provençal herbs with ratatouille and creamy garlic sauce. The restaurant also prides itself on its fresh sea-food selection which always includes mussels and a fresh fish of the day. Hors d'oeuvres, that are almost meals in themselves, plus a superb cheese-board of English farmhouse cheeses completes the picture of the Knife and Cleaver – a cut above the rest! The Knife and Cleaver is a freehouse and offers Adnams Extra Special and Bateman XB Bitter. Also available is Stowford Press Traditional draught cider and a draught lager. There is an excellent wine list with a choice of over 20 wines by the glass.

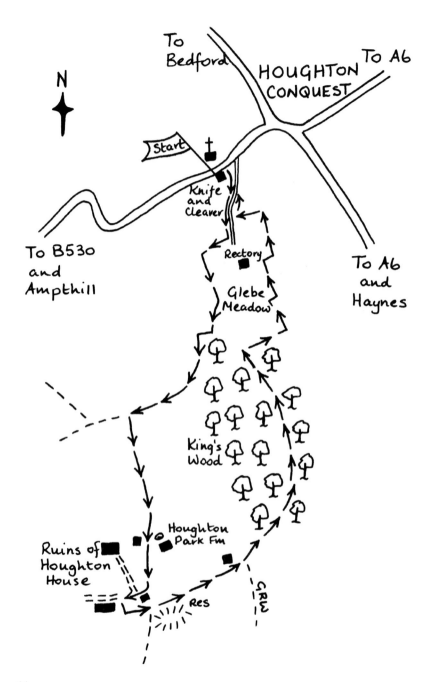

To Bedford

HOUGHTON CONQUEST

To A6

N

Start

Knife and Cleaver

To B530 and Ampthill

Rectory

Glebe Meadow

To A6 and Haynes

King's Wood

Ruins of Houghton House

Houghton Park Fm

Res

GRW

The opening times are Monday to Saturday from 11 am to 3 pm and 7 pm to 11 pm, and on Sundays from noon to 3 pm (closed on Sunday evenings).

Telephone: (01234) 740387.

How to get there: Houghton Conquest is located 4 miles south of Bedford, close to Ampthill, between the A6(T) (Bedford/Luton) and the B530 (Bedford/Ampthill). The Knife and Cleaver is directly opposite the church.

Parking: There is a car park to the front and right-hand side of the pub.

Length of the walk: 4 miles. OS map Landranger series 153 Bedford, Huntingdon and surrounding area; Explorer 208 Bedford and St Neots (GR 044413).

A walk up to the ruins of Houghton House on the Greensand Ridge, John Bunyan's 'House Beautiful'. From here, the route is along the ridge, with wide views over Marston Vale, Bunyan's 'Slough of Despond'. The return path runs through ancient woodland and across meadows rich in wild flowers, now established as an official Local Nature Reserve. (Paths can be muddy – change of footwear advised in winter.)

The Walk

From the Knife and Cleaver the route turns right, across the forecourt, and right again, on an alleyway which runs past the left-hand side of the building. At the end of the alley it turns right, along a back street leading to the Old Rectory. Past the Methodist church it continues ahead until the last bungalow on the left, opposite which it turns right on a fenced-off path leading to Houghton Conquest Meadows and King's Wood. Through a swing-gate the route turns left along a path leading to another gate, where it joins a broad track up to the boundary of Glebe Meadows Nature Reserve, an SSSI (Site of Special Scientific Interest), owned and managed by Bedfordshire County Council.

Just before the wooden gate ahead the route turns right, through a swing-gate, to follow a path running along the edge of the reserve. Over a stile it follows a headland path to the corner of the field where it turns right, then left over a footbridge, now in company with a Marston Vale Timberland Trail. The path runs uphill on the edge of the wood which it leaves as it descends to the right of a hedge. Eventually the path turns left, over a footbridge on the other side of which it keeps ahead following a hedge and ditch. Over another footbridge it runs uphill across an arable field before passing through a swing-gate and up a grassy slope.

Through a gateway to the right of a pond, the route continues up to the top of the ridge on a concrete driveway. Just before the large barn on the left is reached, a gated footpath on the right leads back down the ridge to the ruins of Houghton House. Prior to its destruction it was immortalised as 'House Beautiful' in Bunyan's *The Pilgrim's Progress*. The panelling in the bar of the Knife and Cleaver is thought to have come from the gutted house.

Having rejoined the route after Houghton House, the path continues past the large barn and turns left, just before the line of houses, along the Greensand Ridge Walk (GRW). Past the end of the houses, the track turns left parallel with the reservoir on the right and along the ridge, with wide views across Marston Vale to the north. Past a farmhouse at the end of the track, it enters King's Wood, an ancient woodland now incorporated into the Marston Vale Community Forest.

Just inside the wood the route takes the main, right-hand path, which runs for nearly a mile and at first keeps just inside the edge of the trees. Where the wood eventually extends to the right, the route keeps ahead, ignoring other paths coming in from the left. Eventually the path runs downhill and arrrives at the further end of the wood and a gate into Glebe Meadows. Through the gate the route turns right and follows the hedge to the corner of the first meadow. Here a metal gate leads to a second meadow and the path continues to the corner, where it turns left, heading for the Old Rectory. Just before the boundary fence is reached, it turns right, through a swing-gate and then left along a headland path.

The path keeps to the right of a hedge, past the Old Rectory, for some distance before turning left on a fenced path to the road walked earlier. Here the walk turns right and the route is re-traced back to the Knife and Cleaver.

16 Pegsdon
The Live and Let Live

Pegsdon is a small hamlet just inside the Bedfordshire border with Hertfordshire, nestling at the bottom of Deacon Hill which, together with the Pegsdon Hills, makes it an ideal area for walkers.

The Live and Let Live is remarkable in more ways than one. As a 'born again' pub its past fortunes could be described as 'mixed'. Originally the haunt of local poachers, in 1811 is was besieged by Revenue Men who only got the better of the poachers by piling bales of burning straw against the walls of the pub. In more recent times the pub's good fortunes have been restored following major rebuilding and refurbishment and it now has all the attributes of a good, country pub. The bar area is open-plan with a stone flagged floor and wooden beams. Rugs in front of the open fire and cottage style wooden furniture create a cosy ambience in which to enjoy a quiet pint – music and games machines are banned! The dining area is part quarry tiled, part carpeted with its own open fire and wide bow window overlooking Deacon Hill.

The extensive snack menu includes traditional favourites such as home-made pies, whilst a full à la carte menu is accompanied by a choice of over thirty wines. Grilled fresh fish is the chef's speciality and all meals are served with local vegetables. In addition a set three course lunch is available at a very reasonable price.

The Live and Let Live is a free house currently serving John Smiths Bitter, Marstons Pedigree, Courage Directors Bitter and a guest beer. Guinness, lager and cider are also available on draught.

The opening times are Monday to Saturday 11 am to 11 pm and Sunday noon to 10.30 pm.

Telephone (01582) 881739.

How to get there: Pegsdon is 3 miles north-east of Luton on the B655 between Hitchin and Barton-le-Clay.

Parking: There is a large car park to the rear of the pub.

Length of the walk: 3½ miles. OS map Landranger series 166 Luton, Hertford and surrounding area; Explorer 193 Luton and Stevenage (GR 122303).

This walk to the top of Deacon Hill and Pegsdon Hills provides some of the best panoramic views in the county. It would be no exaggeration to say that people often drive hundreds of miles for views half as good as these!

The Walk

From the pub the walk turns right and follows the lane for a short distance before turning left, along Pegsdon Way which soon becomes a drive leading to Pegsdon Common Farm.

Along this drive there are good views of the line of hills soon to be climbed and well before the farm is reached the walk turns right, following a field-path leading to the base of the hill. Up a flight of steps and across a grassy track it continues ahead with a dry valley to the right and fir trees to the left. This area and the dry valley below once supported a huge colony of rabbits but today only a few remain as a reminder of happier days – for them, anyway! The route turns left at a way-marked post and continues along a 'roller-coaster' stretch of grassy path with good views ahead – notice the outline of Knocking Knoll Long Barrow ahead and to the right. Eventually the path meets a track along which the walk turns right, up the hill. Almost at the top, past the end of a gate, it turns left along a good track for a short distance before turning right at a way-marked post following a headland path to the right of a hedge. Now in company with the Icknield Way (see Introduction for details) it continues down to the road which is crossed over to follow the grassy verge to the right. At the small car park the walk takes the stile to the right of the Icknield

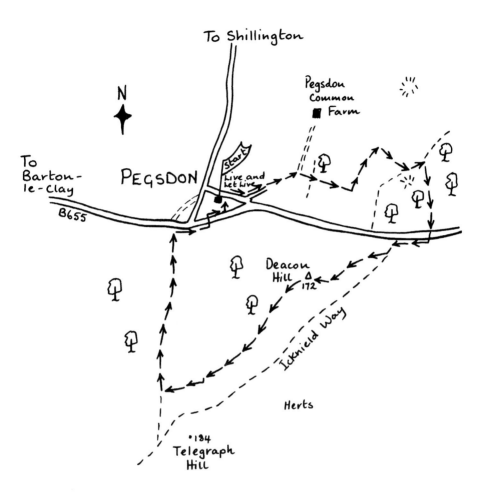

Way over which it continues ahead across open grassland heading for another stile in the distant hedge. Over this it heads diagonally right to climb up the trig point at the top of Deacon Hill (172 metres above sea-level). Stunning 180 degree views open up along the line of the hills and across the landscape below. The Live and Let Live can clearly be seen and is rarely out of sight during the second half of the walk.

From the trig point the walk turns left, along the line of the hills. The path keeps ahead as it runs up and down keeping to the left of the occasional tree or bush. Eventually it meets a stile under overhanging beech trees. Over the stile, the path leads round the top end of a small dry valley and then back up to the top of the hill skirting the edge of a much larger dry valley to the right. Through a swing-gate it keeps roughly ahead before following a fence on the right. Across to the left can be seen an information board which gives full details of this area of the Pegsdon Hills now owned and managed by The Wildlife Trust. Previously ploughed land in this area is being restored to grassland since the surrounding chalk hillsides support many species of wildflower now rare in Bedfordshire. From here the walk keeps to the left of the fence running downhill before passing through another swing-gate and wooded area, on the other side of which it continues ahead, downhill. Eventually, just before the road is reached at the bottom of the hill, the path turns right, inside the fence, which is followed to a last swing-gate. Across the road the walk turns right along the roadside path back to the pub.

⑰ Clophill
The Stone Jug

Clophill is an attractive place with a central green, village lock-up and pound. Georgian houses and 17th and 18th century cottages line its High Street which is well worth a stroll along – look, in particular, for Mill House and Clophill House.

The Stone Jug is located on the northern fringes of the village towards the Greensand Ridge. Built of the local greensand stone, or ironstone, it was originally used for farmworkers and only later converted for use as a pub. Today, it is an honest-to-goodness 'local', with a reputation that extends beyond the village for well kept ale and good food. Inside, a U-shaped bar serves two snug, open-plan areas, complete with open fires in winter. An area for darts is separate at one end, and a small families/dining-room at the other. A range of home-made traditional pub meals, such as Irish tavern pies (beef cooked in stout), is available, plus bar snacks – the bacon and mushroom sandwiches are very popular. Hot food is served at lunchtimes only and not on Sundays. Children are welcome in the family room, but it is probably a good idea to phone in advance as space is limited. Well behaved dogs are allowed in the bar. The Stone Jug is a freehouse,

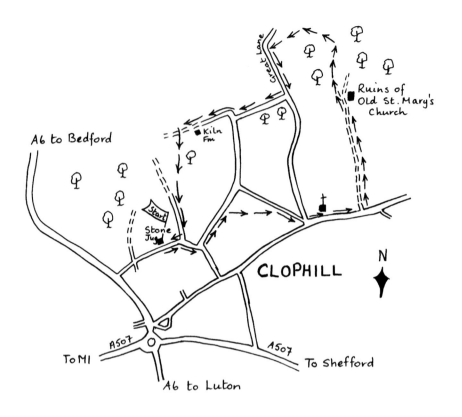

serving John Smith's Yorkshire Bitter, Courage Best, B&T Shefford Bitter, plus two guest beers that change regularly. Guinness, cider and lager are also available on draught.

The opening times are Monday to Thursday from noon to 4 pm and 6 pm to 11 pm, Friday noon to 11 pm, Saturday from 11 am to 11 pm and on Sunday from noon to 10.30 pm.

Telephone: (01525) 860526.

How to get there: Clophill is off the roundabout junction of the A6 (Bedford/Luton) and A507 (Ampthill/Shefford). From the roundabout, follow the A6 north, towards Deadman's Hill. Take the second right along Back Street. The pub is a few hundred yards along on the left.

74

Parking Limited parking next to the pub. It would be considerate, therefore, to consult the landlord before setting out on the walk.

Length of the walk: 3 miles. OS map Landranger 153 Bedford, Huntingdon; Explorer 193 Luton and Stevenage (GR 082381).

A walk which includes upland views to the south and an atmospheric, abandoned church, the ruined square tower of which dominates Deadman's Hill and makes a prominent landmark.

The Walk

From the pub the route turns left, along the road and right at the T-junction. At the next T-junction it turns left, up a short hill and past the village hall to turn right at the second of two fingerposts. The fenced-in path leads down past a stables and skirts a small paddock before ending at a stile on the left. Over the stile the route follows a field-path diagonally right, downhill and across rough pasture, on the other side of which it leads down a bank to a lane. Here the route turns right, past a thatched cottage and along the lane to a road junction where it turns left, to take the road past the front of the church.

New St Mary's church is passed on the left, standing opposite some attractive, older houses and buildings. The church was built in 1848 after the original church on the hill was finally abandoned. Timber from old St Mary's has been used to create a chapel in new St Mary's and the lychgate from the old church can be seen where it now stands in the graveyard in front of the newer church.

After the church, the roadside path continues past the usual mix of old cottages and newer bungalows. A short distance along the road, opposite the small, thatched cottage, the route turns left, along a track leading up to the old church. Where the houses on the left end, the track climbs uphill and there is a good view of the countryside to the south across the valley of the river Flit to the pale blue line of the distant Chilterns.

At the top of the hill the track arrives at the ruin of the abandoned church. This does not wear the past lightly, but broods over land where once stood much of the original village of Clophill. The Black Death decimated the villagers and the survivors fled to the valley below where the church passed earlier in the walk was built. More recently, in 1963 and 1969, attempts to revive the Black Mass were carried out here, graves were desecrated and their contents used in the performance of black rituals and rites in the nave and on what was the previous altar site. Today, all the gravestones have been removed to the boundary wall, and the graveyard has been cleared as a picnic site.

However, there remains a presence or feeling here and, although a pleasant enough spot on a warm, sunny day, who would care, or dare, to be up here on a dark, stormy night when the wind moans round old St Mary's ruined tower?

From the church, the route joins the Greensand Ridge Walk (GRW), as it continues ahead on the track past the church. Clear of the church, it forks left, along a short track leading to a stile. Over the stile it follows the hedge round rough pasture from which there are fine views across the open countryside to the south. Over another stile in the corner, a headland path skirts a large, arable field and runs downhill to a footbridge over a stream. Here the route leaves the GRW and turns left, along a broad, grassy track leading to a lane along which it goes left. Over a rise and down the other side, the route turns right, along Kiln Lane, and rejoins the GRW. This lane runs past a large orchard on the left before reaching another junction, where the route turns right, along Old Kiln Lane. Past a new house followed by a substantial thatched cottage, the lane becomes first a drive and then a track as it passes Kiln Farm on the left.

About 50 yards or so along the track past Kiln Farm, the route turns left, over a stile. From here it runs past the end of a barn and follows the fence across a narrow field to a stile in the corner. Over this and down steps in the bank another stile gives access to a smallholding – a place that never fails to have something of interest in residence, from precocious pigs to kamikaze cockerels!

The path runs ahead to a swing-gate in the middle of the two-paddock smallholding and on to another on its boundary. From here a short track through a belt of trees emerges at the top of a lane known as The Slade. Down this pleasant, shady lane on the outskirts of the village, the route arrives back at the T-junction where the walk started and where a right turn along the road for a short distance leads back to the pub.

⑱ Ampthill
The Queen's Head

Ampthill is an attractive market town with many fine Georgian buildings and old coaching inns complete with arches and stabling yards to the rear.

The Queen's Head is named after Catherine of Aragon, who, as the painting of her on the front of the pub declares, was 'resident in Ampthill after 1531' – albeit, not from choice! Unlike some of the other pubs in the town, the Queen's Head was not a coaching inn, being originally built as two small brick-built cottages which were knocked into one and successfully converted to a pub in 1879. The essentially 'cottagey' construction and atmosphere has been retained and, until recently, the cottagey ghosts that went with it. Two cosy and completely separate bars provide a homely welcome, whilst a dining area serves generous portions of home-cooked, traditional English pub fare. The pub is well-known for the quality of its succulent steaks and home-made pies. Lunchtime meals are available seven days a week and there is a separate 'no smoking' restaurant. The Queen's Head is a Charles Wells pub, serving their Eagle IPA, Bombardier and a guest beer. There is no garden, but a small area to the front of the pub does provide space for outside seating.

The opening times are Monday to Saturday from noon to 2.30 pm and 5.30 pm to 11 pm, and on Sundays from noon to 3 pm and 7.30 pm to 10.30 pm.

Telephone: (01525) 405016.

How to get there: Ampthill is just off the A507 and is easily reached from Junction 13 of the M1 or from the A6(T) Luton to Bedford road. The Queen's Head is in Woburn Road, close to the centre of the village.

Parking: There is a small roadside car park close to the pub and another, much larger one, off the crossroads in the centre of the town.

Length of the walk: 4 miles (or shorter option). OS map Landranger series 153 Bedford, Huntingdon and surrounding area; Explorer 193 Luton and Stevenage (GR 034381).

A walk full of interest. The route first runs through a nature reserve and one of the few surviving areas of gorseland in the county. After this, it climbs to the top of Ampthill Park for magnificent views and the cross which marks the site of the castle where Catherine of Aragon was imprisoned. The return half of the walk also includes a chance to visit the romantic ruins of Houghton House, reputedly used by John Bunyan as the 'House Beautiful' in his famous allegorical work, 'The Pilgrim's Progress'.

The Walk

From the pub the route turns left along Woburn Road on a roadside path, heading away from the town's centre. Just past the car park it turns left, through an ornamental iron gateway, to follow a bridleway track down an avenue of lime trees known as Alameda Walk. Past a playing field on the right the track continues beyond the war memorial to where a swing-gate gives access to the heathland of a Local Nature Reserve and SSSI (Site of Special Scientific Interest), managed jointly by the Bedfordshire and Cambridgeshire Wildlife Trust.

From the swing-gate a sandy path continues ahead and then turns right at a T-junction next to a clump of silver birch trees. The path eventually enters a more wooded area, passing a row of beech trees behind the rugby clubhouse and playing field on the left. At the road the route crosses over to the left and enters Ampthill Park via a wooden gate. From here the path turns left as it runs along the side of the raised cricket ground with its smart brick-built pavilion. Past the cricket ground, the path runs into the car park, where the route turns right, up to a stile set in the right-hand corner. Over the stile the path

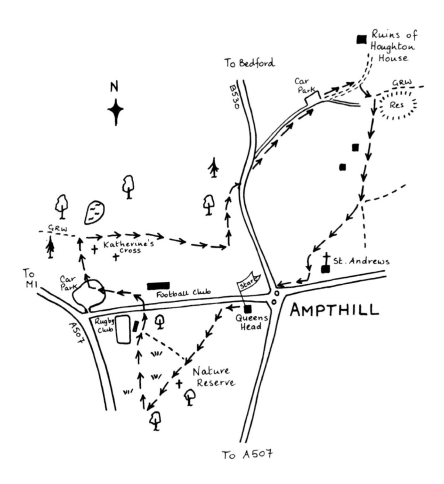

To Bedford

Ruins of Houghton House

N

GRW

Res

Car Park

B530

GRW

Katherine's Cross

St. Andrews

To M1

Car Park

A507

Football Club

Start

AMPTHILL

Rugby Club

Queens Head

Nature Reserve

To A507

runs ahead and uphill to Katherine's Cross. This marks the site of the castle in which Catherine of Aragon, the first of Henry VIII's six wives, was imprisoned pending divorce. More recently the cross was in the national news as the hiding place of buried treasure in a country-wide hunt instigated by Kit Williams in his book, *Masquerade*.

The route crosses diagonally to the left from the stone cross to a view-board with details of what can be seen over the open countryside to the north across Marston Vale. From here the route turns right, along the line of the Greensand Ridge Walk (GRW). Further along the hilltop another stone cross is passed, set back from the path on the right. This cross is the second memorial seen on this walk to the men who died in both world wars. The route continues along the main track, bearing to the left where it forks and a waymarked oak post indicates the line of the GRW. After passing a picnic table and seats in front of a small tree-covered knoll on the right, the track reaches two more waymarked oak posts set fairly close together.

A short-cut can be taken by following the right-hand fork here, which leads down to a house in front of which a driveway leads back down to Woburn Road and the pub. The main route, however, turns left at the second of the oak posts to follow a path through mixed woodland. At a T-junction the route turns right for a short distance on a track which emerges almost at the top of the hill on the road out of Ampthill. Here the route turns left along the roadside path for about 100 yards and, at the crest of the hill, crosses over the road to bear right along a concrete track, clearly signposted to Houghton House. After passing a small car park the track continues along the front of a row of houses. A gated track leads down to the ruins of Houghton House, well worth a visit at this half-way stage of the walk.

Where the houses end, the route turns right, then left past the end of a barn before turning right through the hedge to follow the perimeter fence round a high reservoir. At a fence corner, the path turns right and then downhill left, along the boundary fence and hedge of the farm on the right. Over a stile in the corner, the path continues diagonally right, down and across a pasture, at the bottom of which it turns left along the main drive to the farm. Over a cattle-grid the route turns right, across a footbridge and stile. From here the path runs diagonally left, across a pasture to a stile each side of another footbridge, after which it continues in roughly the same direction across a small paddock.

A V-shaped stile at either end of a short track takes the route to the rear of a church and churchyard. Here it turns right for about 50 yards to a T-junction, where it turns left and arrives at a small square with its attractive almshouses in front of the church. If time permits, visit the church and discover why the American flag is displayed at the altar end.

From the church, the route follows the back street for a short distance down to the main road into Ampthill, along which it turns right. Within a few hundred yards the road runs down to the cross-roads in the centre of the town where the route takes the Woburn road back up to the pub.

19 Ridgmont
The Rose and Crown

Ridgmont is a fairly typical Bedford Estate village in that its houses are largely brick-built and of uniform appearance. Both the church and the pub were built for the estate's workers and the pub remained an estate property until the 1950s. In the 1800s it was also a coaching inn, a connection which was maintained until fairly recently when the annual commemorative coach run from Norwich to Bristol used to change horses here. Inside, the pub has escaped 'modernisation' and has retained its original, separate bars. Pleasantly furnished and very comfortable, each one has a decorative theme, geese in the lounge bar and Rupert Bear in the dining room. Both bars have open fires in winter, which complement the warm welcome in a hostelry with a high reputation for the quality of its home-cooking which has gained a Les Routiers recommendation. There is a delightful garden to the rear where barbecues are held in the summer. The field at the back of the garden provides camping facilities (electricity available).

A good selection of bar meals is available throughout the week. In addition to home made soups, and pies, such as steak and kidney or chicken and mushroom, the Country Griddle specializes in rump,

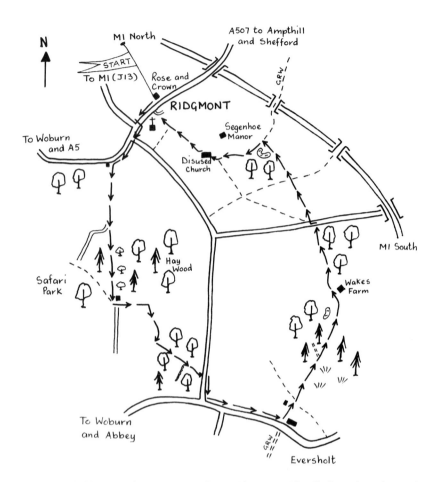

sirloin and fillet steaks up to a 14 oz T-bone with all the trimmings. A selection of king-size country sausages includes Cumberland, pork and onion, curried pork and pork and apple. A full à la carte menu is provided in the completely separate dining-room. This is popular and often full to capacity, so it is advisable to book in advance. As on weekdays the emphasis is on home-cooking using fresh, local produce. The menu changes weekly and currently includes a mouth-watering salmon en croute, and chicken in a special Stilton sauce. Vegetarian dishes are always included. The Rose and Crown is a Charles Wells establishment and winner of their 'Best Real Ale Pub'. Currently on offer is Eagle IPA, Bombardier Best Bitter, Adnams Broadside and a guest real ale. Also available on draught are Guinness, ciders and two lagers.

The opening times are Monday to Saturday from 10.30 am to 2.30 pm and 6 pm to 11 pm, and on Sunday from noon to 3 pm and 7 pm to 10.30 pm.
Telephone: (01525) 280245.

How to get there: Ridgmont is south-east of junction 13 of the M1. It lies on the A507 Shefford road and can also be reached from the A5 Dunstable to Milton Keynes road, taking the A4012 through Woburn.

Parking: There is a car park to the rear of the pub.

Length of the walk: 5 miles. OS map Landranger 153 Bedford, Huntingdon; Explorer 192 Buckingham and Milton Keynes (GR 978363).

A varied walk which includes part of the Woburn Abbey Deer Park and the chance of seeing more exotic animals on the fringes of the Safari Park. The second half covers typical Bedfordshire farmscape plus the ruins of Segenhoe church.

The Walk
From the pub the route turns right, along the very busy Ampthill to Woburn road. The roadside path runs past the Red Lion, followed by All Saints Church, with its empty graveyard, on the other side of the road. The route continues ahead, past the garage, after which, as the road bends right, the route turns left, through the main entrance gates to Woburn Safari Park. A metalled estate road runs ahead through open parkland where various animals, including deer, can be seen throughout the year. (Over 1,000 deer of 9 different species live in the 3,000 acre park, including red deer, sika deer, fallow deer, muntjac deer and milu or Père David's deer. In addition, American bison can usually be spotted in the fields on the right. The Safari Park itself, where over 30 species of wild animals roam 350 acres of parkland, is accessible only by car. It is open daily in the summer months and at weekends during the winter. Telephone: (0525) 290407.

At a T-junction, the road to the Safari Park turns right but, past the barrier, the route continues to follow the road ahead. The road eventually runs through a more heavily wooded area of mixed trees, including rhododendrons and the occasional mature Wellingtonia on the left, and a plantation of new trees on the right. Eventually, Trusslers Lodge is reached where, having crossed the cattle-grid, the route turns left, along a path following the woodland perimeter fence.

In the corner of the field the route turns right and continues to follow the fence until a small wood is reached, where it turns left at a wooden gate. From here a wide track runs just inside the edge of the wood and down to a four-step stile over a fence. Through a belt of trees the path emerges on the left-hand side of an arable field, from where it follows the hedge down to a white gate. Through the gate the route turns right on a narrow lane leading down to a T-junction, where it turns left, along the roadside verge.

The route stays with the road ahead for a good distance before turning off left, along the Greensand Ridge Walk (GRW). The track runs past the end of a line of Bedford Estate cottages and up the rise ahead, past a farmhouse on the left. It then dips down again before bearing right, up through the woods covering a Greensand outcrop. On the other side of the wooded area, the path runs through an open gate and bears left along the edge of the wood, with an arable field to the right. In the corner of the field it passes through a metal gate on a path to the right of a pond or moat. Over a short pasture the path bears left. Through another gate a track is followed behind a red-brick barn and bears left, past the end of a second barn. Clear of the farm it bears right, on a track down the left-hand side of a wood, into a wide valley, with good views across typical Bedfordshire farmscape. Where the track meets the road, the route dog-legs across to take a track leading up the other side of the valley, with the sound of the M1's traffic in evidence.

At the top of the rise, the route continues over a cross-track to follow a headland path along the right-hand side of a hedge. In the corner of the field, it climbs over a stile, next to the remains of another ancient moat. Over the stile it parts company with the GRW as it turns left, along the edge of the wood. From a stile in the corner of the field, the path bears diagonally right, across another pasture and stile, with a good view of Segenhoe Manor to the right. The path continues ahead, aiming to the left of the tower of Old Segenhoe church to a final stile into the rear of the churchyard.

This ruined church of chancel and aisle-less nave dates from the 12th century. It was much altered over the years prior to its abandonment, which was caused by the Duke of Bedford building a replacement more to his liking in the village of Ridgmont. Unlike the church, the churchyard is still in use, and not just as a graveyard, since it is frequented by geese, ducks and even the occasional peacock from the neighbouring farmyard.

Through the roofless church and down to the front of the churchyard, the route leaves via a stile and gate to follow a metalled path back to the road. At the road it turns right for the short distance back to the Rose and Crown.

Shillington
20 The Crown

Shillington spreads itself over a wide area, with the church at its centre. The Crown was purpose built around 1650 and has remained largely unaltered in terms of additions or extensions. Inside, a warm welcome awaits in tastefully decorated, open-plan areas, served by a long bar. At one end is a huge inglenook fireplace and the winter log fires, here and in the lounge, off which there is a separate dining area, create a snug and homely atmosphere. Outside, there is a large garden and a children's play area.

A food-oriented pub complete with separate restaurant, the à la carte menu lists a wide choice of traditional, home-cooked English country fare. In addition, chalkboard menus are changed daily and currently on offer are no less than 10 starters, 14 main dishes and over 20 bar snacks . Grilled mussels with tomato and chilli sauce are a speciality as are the home-made sweets. The Crown is a Whitbread pub and has six cask beers on offer, including Greene King IPA, Morland Old Speckled Hen, Wadworth 6X, Boddingtons Bitter, Fullers Chiswick and Wethered IPA. Guinness, Murphys, Flowers Best Bitter, lager and cider are also available on draught.

The opening hours are Monday to Saturday from 11.30 am to 11 pm, and on Sunday all day, from 11 am to 10.30 pm.

Telephone: (01462) 711667.

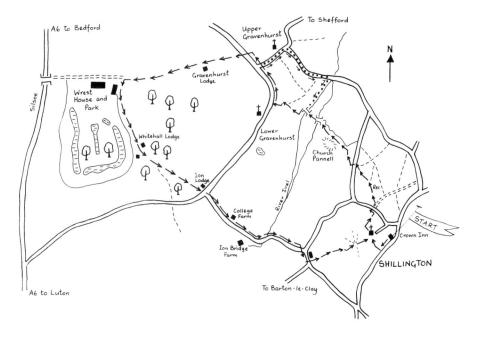

How to get there: Shillington is 6 miles north-east of Luton, midway between the A6(T) Luton to Bedford road and the A600 Hitchin to Shefford road. The Crown is east of the village in High Road.

Parking: There is a car park to one side, and in front of, the pub.

Length of the walk: 5 miles (or shorter option). OS map Landranger series 166 Luton, Hertford and surrounding area; Explorer 193 Luton and Stevenage (GR 127339).

A delightfully rural walk along field paths to the village of Upper Gravenhurst. From here the route follows a ridge-track to Wrest Park House and then another track leads across arable farmland to a quiet country lane, after which a last track leads back to the village.

The Walk
From the pub the route turns right along the roadside path. After passing a cul-de-sac and then a roadside seat, it turns right, over a footbridge. From here a path leads up to the church in the centre of the village. The route crosses the lane, goes up the steps to the churchyard and takes the path to the right of the church.

All Saints stands on a commanding knoll from which there are wide views over the surrounding countryside. The main body of the church was built of local ironstone in the 14th century. However, its original tower was replaced by one built of brick – not a happy marriage! The route leaves from the right-hand, rear corner of the churchyard, through an iron swing-gate. Look for the waymarked circular path signs which this walk follows for most of the way.

At the end of the allotments on the left, the route turns right, down to the road. Here it turns left for a short distance to a crossroads, and crosses over the road to a track past the end of a row of houses. After a few yards, the route turns left, through a metal swing-gate, along a path across rough pasture behind the houses. Another swing-gate in the corner takes the path to a playing field which is crossed straight over. Down a bank on the other side, and through another gate, the route takes the left-hand fork and continues across rough pasture, heading for a stile in the corner of the field. From here it follows the hedge-line to a roadside stile, over which the road is crossed to pick up a track. Over the stream the route turns right, over a stile, to follow a path across the field behind a row of houses. Where the houses end, another stile takes the path across a track to follow the left-hand bank of the stream. The path stays with the stream for some distance before passing earthworks on the left known as Church Pannell, all that remains of a medieval building that once stood on this site.

Eventually, the path crosses two concrete footbridges, one each side of a narrow field. After the second bridge, it turns left along the right-hand bank of the river Ivel for a few yards. At a ditch the path turns right to follow a headland path around the edge of a large arable field. At the boundary corner of the field it switches to the other side of the hedge via a gap and continues ahead and up to the road. Close to the road on the left stands the now isolated church of St Mary. Musket-ball holes can be seen in the doors of the church, which was besieged in the Civil War when local residents sought sanctuary within its walls. The route turns right, along the road and up the hill through Upper Gravenhurst, where, at a T-junction, the main route continues ahead.

A short-cut can be taken by turning right, along the road, and following the waymarked path for 'Circular Walk No 2', which leads back to Shillington.

Almost at the top of the hill the main route turns left, off the road on a bridle track which runs for almost a mile along the line of the ridge. There are good views across the countryside on both sides of the ridge before the track runs down and past a lodge on the left. After climbing again the track gradually descends to Wrest Park House, seen ahead for some time now. Just before the visitors' car park is reached, the route turns left, along a track in front of agricultural buildings.

If visiting the house and grounds, carry on ahead for the main visitors' entrance. Maintained and managed by English Heritage, parts of Wrest Park House, and most of the grounds, are open to the public between April and October, at weekends only. Built in the early 1800s in the French château style as the home of the De Grey family, its grounds are extensive and well worth a visit. Special events are held from time to time, such as falconry displays and a day when the 18th century is brought to life – people in period costume stroll in the grounds and red-coats display the ear-cracking fire-power of muskets and cannon. Telephone: (0525) 860152.

Having turned left, the track runs past the car park and in front of the agricultural buildings. Where the buildings end, the track continues ahead through an open gateway. From here it runs over wide arable fields, with the gardens to the rear of Wrest Park contained by a wide ditch and wall (known as a ha-ha). After passing Whitehall Lodge on the left, the track crosses over a stream, which it then follows just inside woodland. A waymarked post on the right indicates where the circular walk leaves the track, but the route keeps ahead, along the track until it meets the road next to Ion Lodge. Here it crosses straight over, to follow a quiet country lane for a good ½ mile.

The lane provides easy walking with little traffic as it goes over flat farmland each side of the river Ivel crossed earlier in this walk. Past a poultry farm, the river is crossed again as Shillington and its church come into view across the fields. After passing the Shillington village sign, a T-junction is reached, where the route turns right. Past the large, black barns, it turns left, on a bridleway which begins as a drive along the front of some houses. In front of the last house it goes through a wooden gate and down the right-hand side of a pasture. Another gate on the right leads to a short muddy stretch of track which soon changes to a headland path. The path turns left, through a gap in the hedge and over a footbridge. From here the path continues ahead, past a 'spaghetti junction' of footpaths and up the hill to return to the church. From here the route is retraced, back to the pub.

㉑ Woburn
The Black Horse

With over 200 listed buildings, Woburn, with its largely Georgian character and proximity to Woburn Abbey and the Safari Park, make it a popular choice for visitors. During the summer months, a visit to the Heritage Centre and Tourist Information Point in Old St Mary's church is sure to prove rewarding. The Centre is in Bedford Street where there are many fine examples of Georgian buildings, little changed over the years.

Almost opposite is the Black Horse, a 16th century coaching inn complete with coaching arch. Inside, one long bar serves a spacious, open-plan bar divided from a restaurant area at one end of which is the Forge Grill. The Black Horse is an award winning pub with a wide reputation for the quality of its food – especially steaks. The emphasis is on freshness, including sea-food and oysters and the pub was the initiator of Woburn's Oyster Festival; the village's most successful annual weekend event. As a freehouse, over twenty real ales have been on offer in the past. Currently being served are Fuller's London Pride, Courage Directors and a guest real ale. Guinness, lager and cider are also available on draught. A courtyard to one side of the pub provides a pleasant outdoor seating area in fine weather.

The opening times are Monday to Saturday from 11 am to 11 pm and on Sunday from noon to 10.30 pm.

Telephone: (01525) 290210.

How to get there: Woburn is about 3 miles south of Junction 13 on the M1. It can also be reached by turning off the A5 (Dunstable – Milton Keynes road) at the new bypass round Little Brickhill.

Parking: There is a large free car park in nearby Park Street.

Length of the walk: 2½ miles. OS map Landranger series 165 Aylesbury and Leighton Buzzard area; Explorer 192 Buckingham and Milton Keynes (GR 949334).

A short walk full of interest starting as it does in one of the most photographed and painted villages in the county. With distant views of Woburn Abbey in its beautiful parkland setting complete with deer, this stroll has more to offer than many walks twice its length.

The Walk

From the Black Horse the walk turns left, along Bedford Street, up to the crossroads. On the other side of the road the cobbled area is known as The Pitchings, the site of medieval fairs in the distant past. Having crossed over the top end of Park Street, the Bedford Arms Hotel is passed as the walk continues up George Street. After the thatched Royal Oak on the other side, the road crosses Wayn Close, a long, grassy drive once used to connect Woburn Abbey with nearby Maryland, built in the early 1900s by the Duchess Mary as a cottage hospital which provided free medical care for the residents of the village.

At Ivy Lodge the walk joins the Greensand Ridge Walk (GRW) for a short distance as it turns left, through a metal swing-gate along a fenced and sometimes muddy path. Another swing-gate at the end of this path marks the entrance to Woburn Deer Park. Nine species of deer roam freely in the park one of which, the Pere David, was saved from extinction at Woburn.

Through the gate the walk leaves the GRW as it turns left, following the boundary fence to the park. On this stretch of the walk the distant, west face of Woburn Abbey can be seen across the park. (For a closer look, see Walk 25.) This area in front of the Abbey was used as a landing ground by the pre-war 'Flying Duchess' who took up flying at a time when most would be looking forward to a quiet life and

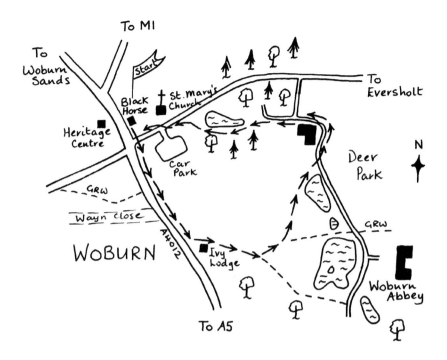

retirement! In honour of her memory there is an annual gathering in August of de Havilland aircraft, including Moths, a type much favoured by the Duchess who gained her pilot's licence flying a Puss Moth. The sight and sound of so many bi-planes in the sky and on the ground in front of the Abbey is an unforgettable experience! Telephone: (01525) 290666.

The grassy path becomes a track as it continues ahead down the side of one of a series of lakes or 'balancing' ponds landscaped by Humphrey Repton in the 1800s. Where the track meets the estate road used as the main vehicular entrance for visitors to the Abbey, the walk keeps ahead, past 'Cowman's Cottage'. Through the main entrance it stays with the road which bends left before passing in front of the Bloomsbury Stud and the estate offices set back across a lawned area. The walk leaves this road as it bends right to cross a cattle grid and follows another road past pretty cottages, with an imposing mini-mansion on the right. As the road turns right, a path is followed ahead past mature trees and rhododendrons before passing yet another large lake, part of the 'balancing' system referred to earlier. The path continues up to Lion Lodge, one of the main entrances to the park, after which a roadside path continues along Park Street, back to the car park, or pub.

Opposite the car park is new St Mary's church built in 1865 by the 9th Duke of Bedford. A huge crypt below the church designed to house the mortal remains of succeeding generations of the Russell family remains empty to this day and has recently been converted to other, more practical uses. Before leaving have a look at the top of the church tower. The tower once supported a lofty spire which became unsafe and had to be removed. It was replaced at the corners of the tower by the present three grotesques, one of which is said to keep a baleful eye on the congregation, one on the church-wardens and the other on the vicar!

㉒ Pulloxhill
The Cross Keys

Pulloxhill is situated on high ground with the Lower Greensand Ridge to the north and the Chiltern Hills to the south. The village has a church, two pubs and several substantial farm houses in its main street with a large water tower at its northern end which provides a well-known landmark in the surrounding countryside.

The Cross Keys is a listed building dating back to the 1600s when it would have been an ale house serving a small, tight-knit rural community. Today it has built up a much wider appeal making it a favourite meeting place for those in search of excellent home-cooking with a wine list to match and/or a good pint of real ale. Outside during the summer months hanging baskets of flowers add to the attractive appearance of the building whilst inside the low, beamed ceilings, small rooms and an ingle-nook fireplace provide a snug setting for the bar. An extension to the rear of the pub provides a restaurant that prides itself on the variety and value for money of its home cooked meals. Grilled steaks, roasts, pies and fish are all served with fresh vegetables in addition to which there is a choice of over a dozen snack meals, such as Drayman's Grill or Virginia Ham. Sunday lunches include a choice of three roasts and are so popular

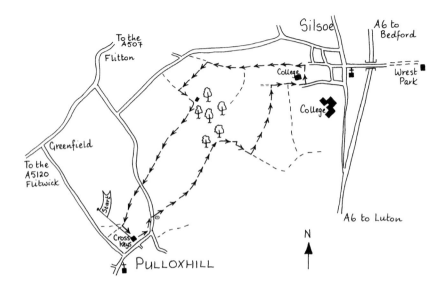

that booking in advance is advisable. There is also a selection of vegetarian dishes.

The Cross Keys is a Charles Wells house and serves their Eagle IPA Bombardier plus Adnams Broadside. Guinness, two lagers and cider are also available on draught.

There are picnic style tables and benches in front of the pub whilst to the rear there is a garden, a pitch for petanque and a children's play area. In addition, acres of mown grassland provide more than enough space for anything from cricket to camping – the latter only by prior arrangement with the landlord who takes much pride in an establishment that has been under his personal supervision for over thirty years!

The opening times are Monday to Saturday from 11 am to 3 pm and 6 pm to 11 pm and on Sunday from noon to 3 pm and 7 pm to 10.30 pm.

Telephone: (01525) 712442.

How to get there: Pulloxhill is 2 miles east of Flitwick between the A6 (Bedford to Luton), the A507 (Ampthill to Shefford) and the A5120 (Toddington to Ampthill) roads. The pub is on the High Street towards the southern end of the village.

Parking: There is a car park behind the pub.

Length of the walk: 4½ miles. OS map Landranger 153 Bedford, Huntingdon; Explorer 193 Luton and Stevenage (GR 063341).

A walk to the nearby village of Silsoe and back. The outward leg provides particularly fine views of the Chiltern Hills to the south, (Bunyan's 'Delectable Mountains'). Silsoe itself is well worth exploring and nearby Wrest Park (open weekends and Bank Holidays only) has one of the best formal gardens of their kind in all England. The environs of Silsoe Agricultural College (plus a chance to visit a car boot sale en route on Sundays in the summer) provide additional interest to a walk that already has much to offer.

The Walk

From the front of the pub the walk turns left, down to Town Farm on the corner, where it follows the road to the left. After a few hundred yards or so the road is crossed to a finger-post on the right from which a path runs past a much fished village pond. Through a purpose-built opening in the fence the path keeps ahead on a field edge path with the hedge on the right. After some distance the path leads through a gap to the other side of the hedge which it continues to follow ahead. Further on a footbridge is crossed to the right and from here the path runs uphill to the right of the hedge. At the top it turns right on a good track following the edge of the wood. All along this part of the walk there are wide views to the south of the distant Barton Hills.

The walk stays with the track as it dips down, turning right and then left on a track heading towards Silsoe and the outlying buildings of Silsoe Agricultural College, now part of Cranfield University. On the skyline can be seen the short masts of two wind-pumps and the track keeps more or less ahead until a T-junction is reached where the route turns right. The track becomes a road through the outskirts of the village and the route turns off to the left following a fenced path to the left of a white house. The path opens and becomes a cul-de-sac which leads past several new houses up to another minor road where the walk can be extended by turning right, to the centre of the village and adjoining Wrest Park (see sketch map).

Now owned by English Heritage, Wrest Park is open at the weekends throughout the summer and its 150 acres of formal gardens provide the setting for special events such as concerts and craft festivals. Telephone 01525 860152 (weekends only) for current information.

Silsoe is worthy of a detour in its own right with its white timber framed cottages in the High Street and two good pubs including the George Inn once famous as a coaching inn.

The pub walk, however, turns left on the road leading past glass-houses belonging to the Silsoe Horticultural Centre. The road soon becomes a track which runs past the two wind pumps seen on the skyline earlier in the walk. Good views open up to the south once more as the walk continues to follow the track ahead, ignoring a footpath leading off to the left. Eventually, at the top of a rise, the route turns left at a crosstracks, keeping ahead on the new track until it bends to the left. Here it leaves the track following a path to the right of a fence round a small paddock. Over a footbridge it turns immediately left on another track or drive leading up to two bungalows. Just before the open entrance to the bungalows is reached, the walk crosses to the right, over a stile and follows the hedge to another stile in the corner of the field. Over this the path keeps first to the left of the hedge then to the right, heading in the general direction of the distant water-tower. After some distance another left turn through the hedge leads to a track across an arable field. Where the track bends sharply left, a field path leads off diagonally left, across the crop, heading now to the right of the distant water tower. Eventually the path leads to a roadside stile over which the road is crossed to a gate immediately opposite. Through this the walk follows the track ahead for a short distance before angling off to the left heading for a stile well to the left of a gate on the far side of the field.

Over this, the walk follows the track to the left which runs up one side of the field used as a venue for car boot sales on Sundays during the summer months. Within a short distance the walk turns left again, through a gap in the hedge, back into the large grounds behind the pub.

㉓ Sharpenhoe
The Lynmore

Sharpenhoe comes within the Chilterns Area of Outstanding Natural Beauty. A small hamlet rather than a village, it is fortunate enough to have retained its pub. Built in the early 1800s, the pub originally included a blacksmith's shop and was named 'The Horseshoe'. Following complete refurbishment in 1983, it was renamed with an amalgamation of the forenames of the proprietor's wife and daughter.

The building has been extended and much altered over the years and now provides an interior of character and charm, especially the heavily beamed area that was once the blacksmith's shop and is now the lounge bar. Off the lounge, a new dining-room has been added, complete with its own bar. The pub has established a high reputation for its home-cooked meals and the car park is always full at lunchtimes. Set and à la carte menus offer a wide choice, whilst over a dozen bar snacks include dishes such as 'Sizzling Spanish Tapas' and 'Mama's Home-made Lasagne'. The Lynmore is a freehouse and serves three cask beers – four in the summer. These are Boddingtons Bitter, Flowers IPA, Fuller's London Pride and Adnams Bitter. Whitbread Poacher, Boddingtons Gold, lager and cider are available on draught. There is a small garden, with slides for the children. Dogs are allowed in the bars, but not the dining-room.

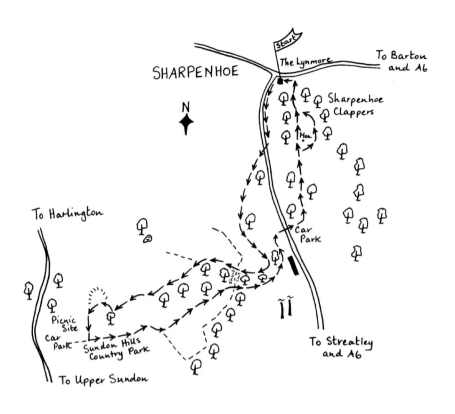

The opening times are Monday to Friday from 11.30 am to 3 pm and 6 pm to 11 pm, Saturday 11.30 am to 3 pm and 6.30 pm to 11 pm and on Sunday from noon to 10.30 pm.
Telephone: (01582) 881233.

How to get there: Sharpenhoe is located between the A6 (Bedford/ Luton) and the M1 (junction 12), north of Luton. The pub is at the crossroads in the centre of the hamlet.

Parking: The car park is next to the pub.

Length of the walk: 5 miles (short-cut available). OS map Landranger series 166 Luton, Hertford and surrounding area; Explorer 193 Luton and Stevenage (GR 064306).

An outstanding walk along the Sundon Hills to the Sharpenhoe Clappers from which can be seen some of the finest views in the county. The term 'Clappers' is derived from the Norman-French word for a rabbit warren, which was built at one end of the earth-works of an iron-age fort situated on top of the hill.

The Walk

From the pub the walk turns left, along the road with a fine view of the hill-top beeches known as the Sharpenhoe Clappers to the left. A good distance up the road the route turns right, through a gate, on a bridlepath running along the base of the wooded slope of the Sundon Hills. After a while the track climbs slightly giving good views over farmland on the right with Pulloxhill water tower prominent on the skyline, (see pub walk number 22). At the T-junction the walk keeps ahead on the track following the bottom of the line of hills. After bearing right for some distance the walk eventually arrives at the National Trust sign for the Moleskin and Markham Hills. Here there is a choice of turning left for the short-cut (see sketch map) or continuing ahead with the main walk.

The main walk stays with the path which keeps to the left of a fence running along the bottom of the hills. Eventually the path stays with the fence as it bears away to the right, down into a dry valley and up the other side. Almost at the top the walk forks left, away from the line of the fence, and climbs to a wooden bench on the brow of the hill. Behind the seat are the old quarry workings, long since grassed over. But on a summer's day the view eastwards from here, along the line of the hills as far as the now distant Clappers, is truly beautiful and ample reward for having walked this far.

From the seat, looking at the distant Clappers, the walk follows a footpath to the right which runs up to a stile next to a gate in the corner. Over this it continues uphill across a sheep pasture aiming for the hedge on the far side, along which it turns left, now in company with the Icknield Way (Scenic Route) and the John Bunyan Trail. (To the right a car park and picnic site marks the main entrance to the park and the start of the John Bunyan Trail.) The walk stays with the hedge and after passing another old quarry to the left goes through a swing gate. The path now skirts the edge of the quarry past which it leaves the long distance paths, (which turn off to the right), as it keeps ahead following the line of a fence down to a steep bank up which a track runs to the left. At the top it bears right to pick up the fence again which is followed down to a makeshift stile in the corner. Over this it keeps ahead along the edge of the bushes before turning diagonally left, through the trees and bushes up another steep bank. At the top it turns left, along another fence, before bearing right at the corner through a cluster of magnificent mature beeches. The path follows the hill top through the woods for some distance before a waymarked post marks where the short-cut rejoins the main route which is also rejoined by the long distance paths.

From here the path keeps ahead for a short distance to another way-marked post. Ignoring any turn-offs to the right it now runs just inside the tree line to the left of a grassy track. Over a stile the path dips down then up to another stile in the fence. Over this it leads across a pasture where the wide views to the left are just a taste of views to come! Over a roadside stile the walk continues ahead through a small car park and past the end of a gate where another National Trust sign marks the entrance to the Sharpenhoe Clappers.

From the car park, the route continues ahead on a metalled track which becomes a field track as it goes through a gate and follows the edge of a wood. At a way-marked oak post the route parts company with the Icknield Way, (Scenic Route), as it bears left through an area of scrub and thorn trees. On the edge of the trees it turns right over an open area with fantastic views below to the left. As the walk enters the beech trees which crown the top of the Clappers, it bears right then ahead, over a bank on the other side of which is the surprising sight of a stone monument set amongst the beech trees - its inscription made all the more poignant by its very unexpectedness . . .

From the memorial, there is a choice of continuing to the left or right around the top of the hill to its far end. Whichever route is taken offers its own attractions and the small effort of circumnavigation is amply rewarded with glorious views in all directions. From the opposite end of the hilltop, just below and outside the beeches, a steep flight of over 150 steps leads back down to a stile on the boundary of the National Trust land. From here a path follows the hedge down to the road where the route turns left, along the roadside path back to the pub.

㉔ Wingfield
The Plough Inn

Wingfield is a small hamlet which, like so many Bedfordshire villages, enjoys a splendid feeling of rural isolation in spite of its proximity to more built up areas. The Plough was built in 1822 as a coaching inn to serve the carriage trade on the nearby main road. Recently re-thatched, its comfortable and homely interior, complete with log burning stove and open fire, has been extended to the rear to include a new dining area. The Plough is a pub that takes its food seriously and offers a wide range of good 'value for money' home cooking. Chalk board specials supplement the extensive bar and à la carte menus and include such succulent dishes as pigeon and apricot pie served with real ale gravy or Haddock Bearnaise served with a creamy white wine and tarragon sauce. Desserts range from Grand Marnier gateau to more conventional favourites such as spotted dick. Two meals for the price of one are on offer from Monday to Friday between the hours of 3 pm and 6 pm. There is a choice for vegetarians and meals are available all day. On Sundays in particular it is advisable to book in advance. There is a pleasant garden behind the pub. Dogs are not allowed inside.

The Plough is a Fuller's pub currently serving five real ales including Fullers London Pride and a guest ale. Guinness, lager and cider are also available on draught.

The opening times are Monday to Saturday from noon to 3 pm and 5.30 pm to 11 pm. Closed on Sunday in winter and open in the summer from noon to 10.30 pm.

Telephone: (01525) 873077.

How to get there: Wingfield is close to Tebworth, just 2 miles south-west of Toddington (junction 12 of the M1). The pub is on the eastern edge of the hamlet and can be reached by minor roads from either the A5(T) (near Hockcliffe), or the A5120 (Toddington to Dunstable).

Parking: There is a car park opposite the pub.

Length of the walk: 3½ miles. OS map Landranger series 166, Luton Hertford and surrounding area; Explorer 193 Luton and Stevenage (GR 002263).

A walk across the fields to the lovingly restored church at Chalgrave, best known for the remains of its medieval wall paintings. Today, the church stands as a fine example of the standards of excellence that can be achieved by a combination of the dedication of volunteers and sympathetic restoration.

The Walk

From the pub the walk turns left, along the road, and follows a section of the waymarked, scenic route of the Icknield Way Path (see *Pub Walks along the Icknield Way Path* by the author of this book). After a short distance the walk turns left, over a stile – look for flint-axe logo – from where it bears right, behind a roadside house as it crosses a sheep pasture to a stile set in the hedge. Over the stile the path, which can be muddy according to the season or recent ploughing, angles left across two wide, arable fields, aiming for a pylon to the right of a gap in the hedge of the first field. Over a footbridge the path continues in the same direction up to the road.

At the busy main road the route turns left for about a hundred yards or so up to a crossroads, where it turns right, along a narrow lane signposted to Chalgrave church. The first of two cottages on the right, Chalgrave Cottage, holds the key to the church, which is kept locked for security reasons. Through the newly-built, small car park at the end of the lane is All Saints church in its peaceful, hill-top setting. The church is all that remains of one of the earliest settlements in Bedfordshire and suffered a long period of neglect following its abandonment. During a storm in 1889, the top section of the tower, then 600 years old, crashed through the roof of the church and lay in ruins in the west bay of the nave for years, bushes and trees growing

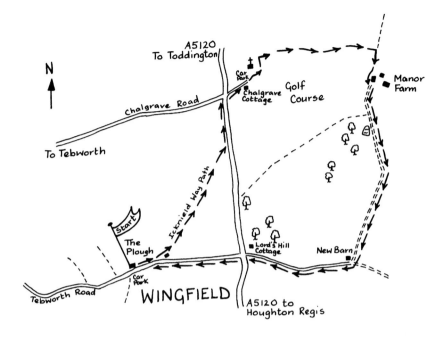

N

A5120
To Toddington

To Tebworth

Chalgrave Road

Car Park

Chalgrave Cottage

Golf Course

Manor Farm

Icknield Way Path

Start

The Plough

Lord's Hill Cottage

New Barn

Car Park

WINGFIELD

Tebworth Road

A5120 to Houghton Regis

among the rubble. Repairs and partial rebuilding allowed the church to re-open in 1931 and the long process of restoration has continued to the present day. Inside there are two good 'table' tombs with effigies plus the remains of the medieval wall paintings, one of the most important features of the church. The paintings range in date from the late 13th to the 18th century. Recent restoration work on the floor of the south aisle uncovered one of the original consecration crosses and a medieval stone coffin lid. The room built in the tower is a fine example of modern craftsmanship at its best. Outside, the churchyard is lovingly tended. Chestnut trees shade wooden seats from which to enjoy views of the church and across open countryside to the south. From the rear of the churchyard, the walk turns right, and follows the hedge as it runs down the left-hand side of a golf course built on what used to be farmland.

At the bottom of the hill the walk parts company with the Icknield Way Path (which turns left), as it turns right, across an arable field to nearby Manor Farm. At the farm buildings the path keeps to the rear of two barns before turning left, then right, along the access road leading to the farm. The road provides a good, all weather surface for the next mile or so as it crosses open, rolling countryside typical of this part of

Bedfordshire. The fields are wide with few hedges and there are good views to the south and west of the distant line of the Chilterns. Past a large pond on the right the road continues up rising ground to New Barn, where it turns right and eventually meets the main road crossed earlier. Over this, Tebworth Road is followed for the short distance back to the pub.

25 Milton Bryan
The Red Lion

Milton Bryan is a small village with attractive buildings both old and new. The row of thatched cottages opposite the Red Lion is as pretty as any to be found in the county and the area around the nearby Town Pond is well worth exploring.

Originally built as a farmhouse in the 17th century, the Red Lion has been sympathetically converted to its present use. The open plan interior has cottagey wooden chairs and tables at one end complemented by a good sized, carpeted dining area at the other. Wooden beams, a partly flagged floor and open fires combine to create the atmosphere of a traditional country pub, a place to relax and enjoy life! In this connection the pub has established an enviable reputation for its meals ranging from home-cooked casseroles and pies to a full à la carte menu. The Red Lion is a Greene King pub currently serving IPA, Ruddles County, HSB Bitter and Morland Old Speckled Hen. Guinness, three lagers and a cider are also available on draught. There is a patio and grassed area to one side of the pub with picnic style benches and seating.

The opening times are Monday to Saturday from 11 am to 3 pm and

6 pm to 11 pm and on Sunday from noon to 4 pm and 6 pm to 10.30 pm.
Telephone: (01525) 210044.

How to get there: Milton Bryan is just off the A4012 between Woburn and the A5(T) Dunstable to Milton Keynes. The pub is at the centre of the village opposite a row of thatched cottages.

Parking: There is a good-sized car park to the front of the pub.

Length of the walk: 5 miles. OS map Landranger series 165 Aylesbury and Leighton Buzzard area; Explorer 192 Buckingham and Milton Keynes (GR 302974).

A walk with much to remember: the magnificent view of the west face of Woburn Abbey across the lake; the deer; Paris House; plus Milton Bryan's hush-hush, wartime secret!

The Walk

From the pub the walk turns right along the roadside path. Past a T-junction it turns right over a stile to the left of the entrance to Leys Farm. Across the top corner of this paddock and through a swing-gate the path leads up to a drive which is followed through Church End to the road. St Peter's church on the right was much restored in the 1840s and contains a stained glass window commemorating Joseph Paxton, designer of the Crystal Palace, who was born in this parish.

Across the road a footpath leads between Bedford Estate cottages, beyond which it keeps ahead on what was once the perimeter path encircling the secret war-time Black Propaganda studios. On this site, inside a wire fence patrolled night and day by guard-dogs and men armed with tommy-guns, German language broadcasts were prepared to give the impression that they came from 'somewhere in occupied Europe'. Every trick of 'disinformation' was used in an attempt to sabotage the German war effort and keep German military personnel glued to their Short Wave sets, whilst the most powerful Medium Wave transmitter in Europe broadcast false news designed to cause chaos and confusion in the civilian population. The day after the war was over all records of Milton Bryan as a propaganda broadcasting station were destroyed. It is now a Scouts' camping ground.

The crumbling concrete path winds left and right and ends with the war-time building in full view to the right. Here the walk turns left on a grassy track down to and through an open gateway where it keeps forward on a headland path. In the corner of the field it turns right on a track running parallel to the wall surrounding Woburn Deer Park.

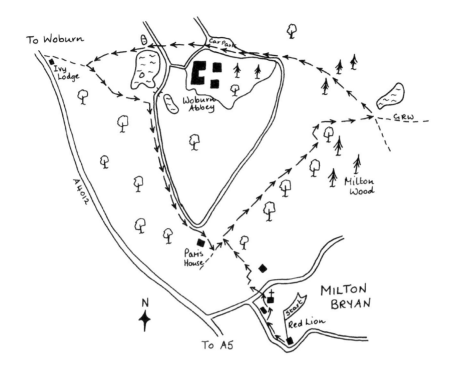

The path keeps ahead through Milton Wood, across rough pasture and over a stile before broadening to a track. Eventually the track bears left and just before the edge of the wood is reached the walk turns off left on a narrow path running down to a footbridge across a stream. From here it keeps ahead across a grassy track keeping to the right of a way-marked oak post. With the stream now on the right the path runs through great bamboo-like clumps before crossing a footbridge over the stream. The path keeps ahead and after a stile, an oak fingerpost marks a meeting of ways where the walk turns sharply left on the Greensand Ridge Walk.

After crossing two more footbridges and a stile it emerges at the bottom of a wide, arable field up the middle of which runs a good track. After dog-legging right, then left through a belt of fir trees, a stile is crossed and the path runs uphill across rough pasture planted with new trees. The deer park is re-entered via a combination stile and swing-gate and the line of the path ahead is marked with low, oak

107

posts. Eventually the path joins the estate road to the rear of Woburn Abbey and the road is followed down past the main entrance.

At this point it is possible to visit the Abbey and/or its gardens. However, to do full justice to the Abbey's many attractions takes several hours and probably justifies a separate visit. Telephone: (01525) 290666.

The walk continues ahead along a road marked 'No Entry' for about 50 yards before following a path running downhill and crossing another estate road. Over the road the path runs alongside a large lake across which can be seen the west face of the Abbey.

The lakeside equestrian statue seen in front of the Abbey stands as a tribute to 'Mrs Moss', in her time a much-loved horse from the Abbey stud.

Past the lake the line of the path is marked by low, oak posts as it runs diagonally across wide, rough pasture to where metal swing-gates provide another entrance to the deer park. Without going through the gates the walk turns left to follow another grassy path through trees to the right of the lake. Following the oak posts the path eventually meets another estate road along which it turns right. The walk stays with the road for some distance as it crosses undulating park land. The walk leaves the road, which turns left, as a path is followed ahead then along the fence around Paris House.

This black and white building is not all it seems. Once part of the Paris Exhibition, the then Duke of Bedford liked it so much that when the exhibition was over he had it dis-assembled, shipped over and re-erected on this site. During the war it saw many illustrious visitors including the King and Queen, General de Gaulle and for a time housed a high ranking SS Officer who 'assisted' with the Black Propaganda broadcasts prepared by Milton Bryan. Paris House is now an expensive restaurant.

The path continues to the estate boundary wall through which it passes via a metal swing-gate. Through the trees it turns left along a headland path to the corner of the field where it joins the outward leg as it turns right. From here the outward route is retraced back to the pub.

Linslade
The Globe Inn

26

The Globe Inn is picturesquely located on the Grand Union Canal and the original farmhouse was converted to a pub after the coming of the canal over 200 years ago. The heavily beamed interior of the inn provides a comfortable and spacious lounge/restaurant, with additional areas for children and two other bars. A large canalside garden is used for summer entertainments, such as live music and barbecues. There is also a children's play area with its own fizzy-drinks and ice-cream bar in the summer.

The restaurant offers delicious home-made cooking, from main courses to desserts. The hot skillet steaks are a house speciality, and the Sunday lunch particularly good value for money. Meals are available seven days a week. The Globe is an Old English Inn Company house with a good choice of real ales, including Greene King Abbot, Ruddles County, Wadworth 6X plus guest ales. Guinness, cider and lager are also available on draught.

The opening times are Monday to Friday from 11 am to 3 pm and 6 pm to 11 pm, Saturday 11 am to 11 pm, and on Sunday from noon to 10.30 pm. In winter, the opening times should be confirmed by phone.

Telephone: (01525) 373338.

How to get there: Linslade is 1 mile north of Leighton Buzzard on the A4146 Milton Keynes road. The turning down to the inn is signposted and descends steeply to a bridge over the canal, from which it can be seen to the right.

Parking: There is a large car park behind the pub.

Length of the walk: 4½ miles (or shorter option). OS map Landranger series 165 Aylesbury and Leighton Buzzard area; Explorer 192 Buckingham and Milton Keynes (GR 913263).

A walk that combines peaceful countryside and views across the valley from the Greensand Ridge, followed by an easy return leg along the canal towpath, from the Three Locks, enlivened by the 'business' of boats and the bustle of waterside activity, with the river Ouzel on the other side of the watermeadows. Go well shod.

The Walk

From the pub the route turns right, along the canal. Just before the bridge is reached it turns right, over a stile waymarked for the start of the Greensand Ridge Walk (GRW). Having crossed the stile, it turns left, down a bank, following the hedge across low-lying meadowland. At the end of the railway sleepers laid across a ditch, it turns right and continues across watermeadows, before turning left along the bank of the river Ouzel.

The walk stays with the river bank for a short distance and then turns right, over the river, on a substantial wooden footbridge. On the other side of the river it bears left and follows the overhead electricity lines up the rise, to where it meets a metalled drive and carries on along it. Across a cattle-grid it turns left along a track, waymarked for the GRW, along the base of the Greensand Ridge. The walk stays ahead until reaching a metal gate leading to the road.

Those who wish to take a short-cut should go through the gate and turn left, along the lane. At a bridge over the Grand Union Canal, it turns left on the canal-side towpath leading back to the pub.

Without passing through the gate the main walk leaves the track as it turns right following the line of the roadside hedge. Where the hedge ends it keeps more or less ahead through woodland bordering the road before angling down to a crossroads. The route now follows the road opposite, signposted to Great Brickhill, to the right of which is the main entrance to Rushmere Park. About 50 yards further on, the route leaves the road, as it turns right through a wooden swing-gate, still

110

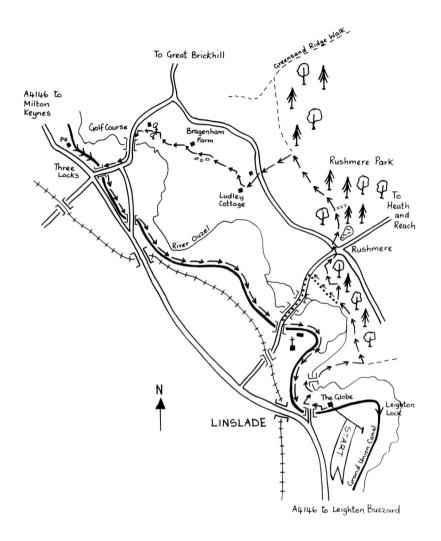

To Great Brickhill

A4146 to
Milton
Keynes

Golf Course

PH

Three
Locks

Bragenham
Farm

Ludley
Cottage

River Ouzel

Greensand Ridge Walk

Rushmere Park

To
Heath
and
Reach

Rushmere

N

LINSLADE

The Globe

Leighton
Lock

START

Grand Union Canal

A4146 to Leighton Buzzard

following the GRW. The path runs past a large lake and giant red-woods on the right, before bearing left, as it begins to climb back up the ridge. Towards the top it bears left at a T-junction before a short, steeper climb, after which it continues along the ridge top, just inside the edge of the trees with good views across the valley to the west.

Further along, a stile is crossed, soon after which the route leaves the ridge and the GRW, as it turns left over a small stile in the fence. From here the path runs ahead and slightly downhill across a wide, arable field to a roadside stile (aim for the waymarked oak post, then keep to the left of the galvanised iron water trough). Across the lane, the route follows a track past a farmhouse and then turns right, just before reaching Ludley Cottage. A few yards down this track it bears right on a path down to a footbridge and stile marked with the white arrow of the Chiltern Ramblers. The white arrow continues for some distance and is an excellent, easily seen marker. From here a path bends right, then almost immediately left, across railway sleepers over a small stream, after which it continues ahead over boggy ground. Clear of the soft ground, the path runs through bracken up a short rise to another stile. A succession of stiles now take the path to the right of ponds created by what look like old sand-pit workings. Past the last pond it crosses a grassy track and bears left, across pasture, to a stile. Over this the path leads through trees and over another stile behind a house before emerging on a small hillside and more rough pasture. From here the path is more difficult to follow as the ground is very boggy in places and the white arrow markers disappear.

From here the route continues ahead following a fence on the left and past a pond on the right. The path angles left to stay with the fence before bearing over boggy ground up to a waymarked (plastic disc) telegraph pole. From the right of the telegraph pole the route continues almost to the top left-hand corner of the field before turning left, through a belt of thorn bushes. After a stile in the fence of a small paddock, the route crosses diagonally left to a metal gate. From here it runs downhill, aiming to the right of a fallen tree in the corner of the field. Over another stile it follows the hedge to a last stile in the corner of the field next to the road.

Here the route turns left, along the road and over the river, past the new golf-course on the right-hand side. At a T-junction it keeps ahead up to the Three Locks bridge over the canal.

From the Three Locks, the route turns back under the bridge, along the towpath. The path runs for more than a mile back to the pub, with easy, pleasant walking and plenty of time to enjoy the canalside scene. Eventually, Manor Farmhouse and the old church of St Mary are seen on the opposite bank. Just after passing the church, now disused and on the Bedfordshire side of the border, bridge No. 111 over the canal is reached, just beyond which is the inn where the walk started.

27 Totternhoe
The Cross Keys

Nearby Totternhoe Knolls is part of the Chiltern Hills, an Area of Outstanding Natural Beauty (AONB). The village is divided into three parts, or 'Ends', with most of the older, half-timbered, thatched houses clustered around Church End and St Giles's church. The name of the village means a hill spur near a lookout, whilst the name of the pub is associated with the religious emblem of St Peter.

The Cross Keys pub nestles at the base of the spur which overlooks the Ouzel valley and is a half-timbered and thatched building dating back to the 15th century. It is a pretty pub, both inside and out, with summertime hanging flower baskets and yellow painted window shutters complementing a beamed, tastefully decorated and comfortable interior. There are two open fireplaces, including a massive inglenook fireplace which is no longer used since it sparked a fire in the thatch in the sixties. A small dining-room is at one end and on offer is a good range of home-cooked meals, all of which are prepared with vegetables supplied fresh from the nearby allotments. Home-made soups and pies are a speciality, with rabbit pie and beef in red wine vying in popularity with succulent steak and kidney puddings. Sandwiches and jacket potatoes are also available with a wide range

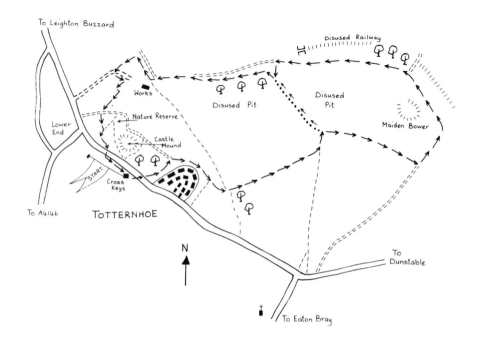

of fillings, including vegetarian ones. The Cross Keys serves Greene King IPA, Wadworth 6X and a guest beer. Guinness, Calders Cream Ale, cider and two lagers are also available on draught. There is a large, pleasant garden with good views, complete with slides and other play equipment for the children.

The opening times are Monday to Saturday from 11.30 am to 3.30 pm and 6 pm to 11 pm (open all day on Saturdays in the summer), and on Sunday from noon to 3.30 pm and 7 pm to 10.30 pm.

Telephone: (01525) 220434.

How to get there: Totternhoe lies 3 miles south-east of Leighton Buzzard and 2 miles west of Dunstable, between the A5 (Dunstable/Milton Keynes) and A4146 (Leighton Buzzard/Hemel Hempstead). The pub is at the northern end of the village (known as Lower End), on Castle Hill Road.

Parking: There is a large car park to the left of the pub.

Length of the walk: 4 miles (short-cut available). OS map Landranger series 165 Aylesbury and Leighton Buzzard area; Explorer 192 Buckingham and Milton Keynes (GR 979219).

114

A varied and interesting walk around the edge of reclaimed quarry workings, with glorious views across to Dunstable Downs, Ivinghoe Beacon and the Chilterns. Further on it passes the site of an Iron Age fort and ends at a nature reserve established round the site of a Norman motte and bailey castle.

This lovely walk is best enjoyed in summer, when the tracks are dry. On wet weather days the circuit around Castle Mound is a good short walk and will give you a taste of the delights of the longer route.

The Walk

The route crosses over the road in front of the pub to follow the public footpath opposite. The path climbs a short rise and then levels out as it runs along the base of the hill behind the houses. Eventually, it climbs more steeply up to where it meets a track and turns right. The first good views open out to the right before the track bears left and continues to a cross-tracks, with the picnic site on the right, in what was once a small chalk quarry. The route keeps ahead, over the cross-tracks. From here it climbs up the hill, close to the edge of a huge disused quarry, the bottom of which has been reclaimed and grassed over.

As the track gains the top of the hill, panoramic views open up in all directions. To the south-east can be seen the line of the Chilterns with the London Gliding Club at the base of the Dunstable Downs. Along the hills to the right is the white outline of the Whipsnade Zoo lion, whilst on a clear day it is possible to see well past Ivinghoe Beacon to the beginnings of faraway Oxfordshire.

At the far end of the quarry, a short-cut can be taken by turning left, on the path which runs along the other edge of the quarry, and down to where it rejoins the return half of the main walk.

The main route turns right on a track or 'white' road. Further along the track, the circular hedge in the field on the left marks the boundary of Maiden Bower, an Iron Age fort (700 BC to AD 43). Eventually, the route turns left on the waymarked Icknield Way, with the housing estates on the outskirts of Dunstable now only a field's distance from the site of the fort. After some distance, the route turns left again, to run downhill, with Maiden Bower now to the left, and the deep cutting of the disused railway line, which once linked Leighton Buzzard and Dunstable, on the right. At a T-junction the route continues ahead, keeping to the left of the woods. After passing an old railway bridge on the right, the track is relinquished in favour of easier walking, where a waymarked oak post indicates a path running uphill. This path is the other end of the short-cut referred to earlier.

A short distance up this path the route turns right, over a stile, and then left to run along the hillside parallel with the track below. After about ¼ mile, the path clears the woodland and stays with a raised, grassy track before a stile where the main track is rejoined. The route now runs ahead to another T-junction, directly in front of the huge, clanking, whirring, steaming, dust-covered 'satanic mills' of the Totternhoe Lime and Stone Company. Here the route turns right and, after about 100 yards, left, along another track which soon becomes a metalled lane. At the main entrance to the works, the route turns left, along a fenced-in path to the right of the gates. This path turns left and right along the edge of a sheep pasture before running up to and straight over another track.

From here the path continues ahead along the line of a new fence as it enters the Totternhoe Knolls Nature Reserve. It then leaves the fence and bears right, down to a more obvious path which it follows left, through an area of the nature reserve known as 'Little Hills'. This area was quarried from at least the early 12th century for its hard chalk-stone or 'clunch', which was used in local buildings, such as churches, and also in famous landmarks, such as Westminster Abbey and Windsor Castle.

About 50 yards along the path, a T-junction is reached with the earthworks of Castle Mound, another area of the reserve, in plain sight ahead. These are the remains of a late 11th or early 12th century motte and bailey, known then as Eglemont (Eagle's Mount), now a scheduled Ancient Monument. The areas of the reserve have been designated a Site of Special Scientific Interest (SSSI), due to the rare chalkland plants to be found here, including seven species of orchid.

At the T-junction in front of Castle Hill, the route turns right, on a path which runs downhill through a beech plantation on the lower slopes of the hill planted about 1870. The path eventually leads to a roadside stile. Over the stile the route turns left along the road and back to the pub.

㉘ Dunstable
The White Swan Inn

Sited at the crossing of the Icknield Way and Watling Street, Dunstable has a long history as an important staging post for travellers.

The White Swan, affectionately known to its regulars as 'the mucky duck', dates back to before 1769, when it was sold and described as 'late The Two Black Boys'. At some time in its history part of the cellar was used as a town lock-up, complete with brick 'bunks' and small iron grills to the pavement above. Today, it is run as a comfortable, town pub by a landlord who takes pride in its success at every level – as witnessed by the numerous sporting trophies on display. Sporting prints also decorate the walls, whilst an open fire puts the finishing touch to a comfortably furnished, open-plan interior.

Home-cooked meals served at lunchtimes include soups, the popular Dirty Duck Delight – a hearty, mixed grill and such dishes as Spanish omelette. A wide variety of sandwiches with generous fillings are regarded as a house speciality. Children are welcome and there is a choice for vegetarians. Meals are not available on Sundays, except for a barbecue during the summer months – weather permitting. There is a pleasant garden to the rear of the pub in spite of its proximity to the town centre. Dogs are not allowed inside.

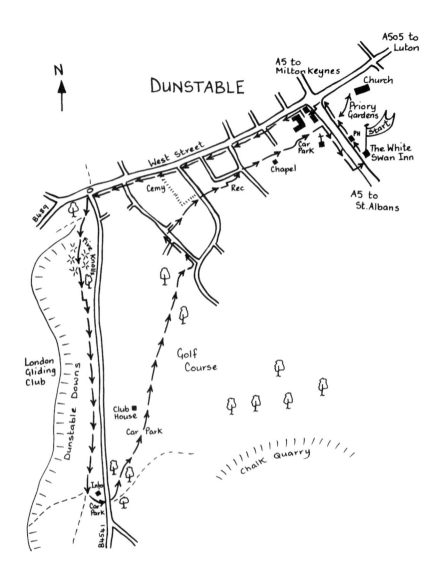

The White Swan is a freehouse and serves Marston's Pedigree Bitter, Boddingtons Bitter, Webster's Yorkshire Bitter and a guest ale, currently Morland Old Speckled Hen. Courage Best Bitter, cider and five lagers are also available on draught.

Opening times are Monday to Saturday 11 am to 11 pm, and on Sunday noon to 10.30 pm.
Telephone: (01582) 667833.

How to get there: Dunstable is on the main A5(T) just west of Luton. The pub is close to the centre of the town on the A5(T), Watling Street.

Parking: There is roadside parking on the slip road in front of the pub.

Length of the walk: 4 miles. OS map Landranger series 166 Luton, Hertford and surrounding area; Explorer 193 Luton and Stevenage (GR 023216).

A walk from the centre of the town, up to and along Dunstable Downs, famous for wide ranging views across Aylesbury Vale and along the line of the Chiltern hills. In addition, the sailplanes of the London Gliding Club provide the best free show in the county. The walk also includes the Five Knolls, a Bronze Age burial site.

The Walk
From the pub the walk turns right, on the pavement along the High Street, heading for the centre of the town. Various houses and buildings of historic interest are passed, including Chew's House, originally a Church of England school for 40 boys, and a row of 18th-century alms houses. Past the Saracen's Head, Dunstable's oldest surviving pub, the entrance to Priory Gardens is reached, inside which stands the Priory Church of St Peter. The church is all that survives of the monastic buildings on this site built by Henry I, around 1131. A view-board in the gardens shows a conjectural view of the church and monastery, which, together with the impressive surviving west face and the scale of the interior, gives more than a hint of former glories.

Past the entrance to the gardens, the walk crosses to the other side of the road via a Pelican crossing, turns left for a few yards, then right, through an arch into a small shopping precinct. Here it turns right again, past the shops to a road, West Street (A505), along which it turns left. This road is followed for some distance as it runs slightly uphill, past two pubs, one each side of the road, and the main entrance to a cemetery before reaching a large roundabout. The route joins the scenic route of the Icknield Way Path (waymarked with a flint-axe logo), as it turns left, up a grassy slope to the left of the roundabout.

Through a swing-gate at the top of the slope it continues ahead over short, springy turf below the road and the crest of the hill. All along this stretch of the Downs there are wide views across Aylesbury Vale and along the line of the Chilterns as far as distant Oxfordshire. Within a short distance the walk passes the Five Knolls, the finest group of

119

Bronze Age burial mounds in the Chilterns. The first mound passed, the site of a gallows in medieval times, was excavated by Sir Mortimer Wheeler before the last war. At the centre a crouched female burial was uncovered, as were the later remains of about thirty bodies buried in rows, with their hands tied behind their backs. The finds are kept in Luton museum.

Beyond the mounds the path bears right as it follows the line of the hill and passes an area to the left used by the hang-gliders that soar straight off the hilltop. Through another swing gate the path leads up to the Dunstable Downs Information Centre and shop, where a small kiosk serves light refreshments. The centre opens every afternoon during the summer (except Mondays); Sundays and bank holidays during the winter. Display boards and leaflets give details of walks and wildlife on the Downs plus information on the surrounding area. With the headquarters of the London Gliding Club at the base of the Downs almost directly below, this is an ideal spot from which to enjoy the view and a cup of tea whilst watching the gliders being winched and towed aloft. A short distance down the slope to the left a large information board displays details of the network of prehistoric tracks, known as the Icknield Way, which stretched all the way from Dorset to the Wash. From here, the walk continues through the car park next to the Centre and crosses the road to the right before turning left, on the historic route of the Icknield Way path into Dunstable. Through bushes and scrub the path emerges on the edge of the upper reaches of Dunstable Downs golf course which is crossed aiming to the right of the clubhouse. Along this stretch there are good views of Blows Down to the right and across Dunstable and Luton. To the north can be seen the Sundon Hills (pub walk 23), to the north-west, the distant Warden Hills (pub walk 29). Past the clubhouse the path continues in roughly the same direction before entering another area of scrub. Eventually, the walk bears left to follow a tarmaced path down to a road.

Here, the route turns left, to a T-junction, and left again for a few hundred yards before turning right on a track between houses and past a cemetery to another road. Across this, it keeps to a path down one side of a recreation field which soon bears left, between houses, to a road junction. Bearing right, over the junction, the walk follows a road past a chapel to a car park, which is skirted right, then left. Past a supermarket on the left it arrives at a T-junction back in the small shopping precinct. Here, it turns right, past the Methodist church, to emerge on the opposite side of the High Street walked earlier. An old inn sign is passed, a reminder of the days when five pubs stood on this side of the High Street between here and the cross-roads. Today, the sign shows an extracted molar. . .! Within a short distance another Pelican crossing is reached, across which the walk arrives back at the pub.

Luton
The Warden

The Warden, named after the nearby hill, is situated on the northern fringes of Luton, Bedfordshire's biggest town. A substantial, 1930s brick building, it once boasted its own dance floor in the days when the Saturday night 'hop' was still eagerly anticipated as the most important social occasion of the entire week.

Today, it belongs to the Beefeater chain, popular both as a local 'watering-hole' and with passing trade on the A6. Spacious, open plan accommodation is comfortably furnished and served by a long bar. The old dance floor area has been converted into a restaurant serving 'good value for money' meals which vary according to the season, but always include such staples as hearty steaks or a variety of fish and chicken dishes. Bar meals include baguettes or jacket potatoes with various fillings, plus pastas or curries. There is a children's menu and a good selection of vegetarian meals. The restaurant is open throughout the week and is often supplemented by a week-end barbecue during the summer. There is a large garden which is well equipped with children's slides etc; dogs are welcome in the garden, but not inside.

Cask ales on offer include Boddingtons Bitter and Flowers Original

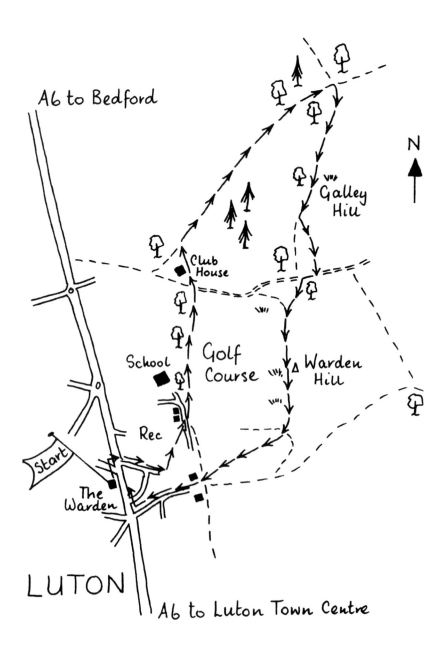

A6 to Bedford

N

Galley
Hill

Club
House

Golf
Course

School

△ Warden
Hill

Rec

Start

The
Warden

LUTON

A6 to Luton Town Centre

plus a guest beer, such as Castle Eden Ale. Guinness, Murphy's, lager and cider are also available on draught.

Opening times are Monday to Saturday from 11 am to 11 pm, and on Sunday from noon to 10.30 pm. Telephone: (01582) 591277.

How to get there: Luton, in southern Bedfordshire, can be reached from J10 or 11 of the M1. The pub is on the A6(T) Luton/Bedford road, on the northern edge of the town.

Parking: Ample parking to the front, side and rear of the pub.

Length of the walk: 4 miles (short-cut available). OS map Landranger series 166 Luton, Hertford and surrounding area; Explorer 193 Luton and Stevenage (GR 083255)

A fine walk with splendid views virtually on the doorstep of the largest conurbation in the county. Go on, surprise yourself...

The Walk

From the pub, the walk crosses over the (A6) and turns left along the road-side path. After fifty yards or so, it turns right, down Hillcrest Avenue. At the end of Hillcrest Avenue, it keeps ahead, through a gap in the hedge and turns left, along a fenced path. Across the end of a recreation field, the path leads to a road in front of houses facing Warden Hill. The walk keeps left as it crosses over the road which is followed to just before a roadside car park and the main entrance to a school. At the information board it keeps ahead to the right of a high hedge with South Bedfordshire Golf Course stretching across to the foot of the hills on the right. The first of several way-marks for the Icknield Way (Rider's Route) is passed before the path eventually crosses over a main track.

Here, a short-cut can be taken by turning right, (see sketch-map), across the golf course and the remains of Iron Age tribal boundaries known as Dray's Ditches.

The main walk, however, keeps ahead and bears left behind a green, after which it joins a wide track running past the front of the club-house. The walk stays with this track ignoring turnings off to the right and left before bearing right as the track begins a long but fairly gradual climb up the hill. After the golf course ends, the track climbs more steeply to reach a cross-tracks, to the left of which is an information board on the Icknield Way, its historical background and overall route.

Here the walk leaves the combined routes of the Icknield Way Path as it turns right along a branch of the Icknield Way designated the

Historic Route, (See *Pub Walks along the Icknield Way Path* by the author of this book).

The path is followed to the right, across the fairway to a swing gate at the bottom of Galley Hill which together with nearby Warden Hill has been designated a Site of Special Scientific Interest (SSSI). Some of the richest grassland for wild flowers is to be found in this area. Management includes the clearance of scrub and the reintroduction of sheep in order to keep growth in cleared areas under control. Dogs must be kept on a lead within these fenced areas.

As the path climbs to the top of the hill good views across open countryside open up behind (north). Bumpy ground and hollows mark the remains of tumuli and the site of the gallows from which the hill gets its name. Excavations in this area have revealed some gruesome finds and indications of black magic rituals. Over the hill the path is followed down to a swing-gate through which the walk continues along a field-edge path with fine views across Luton and more open countryside. In the corner of the field it turns left (do not go through gate), and continues to follow the edge of the field until meeting a track. Here it joins the Bunyan Trail as it turns right on a track running downhill. Within a short distance it turns left, with the Bunyan Trail, through a swing-gate, at which point the short-cut joins the main walk. From here the path runs uphill again to the top of Warden Hill where it keeps roughly ahead before bearing left to another gate. Through this it keeps to the right of a wire fence with wide views to the right, including ground below covered in the earlier stages of the walk. A trig point (around 600 feet above sea level) on the other side of the fence, provides an excellent vantage point from which to enjoy wide views that stretch to the easily recognizable control tower at Luton airport, on the horizon to the south-east. Past the trig point the walk continues to follow the fence and where this ends the path keeps more or less ahead, down to a grassy knoll. From here there is a choice of paths, all of which run down to the bottom of the hill. This walk follows the left-hand of two paths which leads downhill quite steeply to another swing-gate through which it continues ahead over rough pasture at the bottom of the hill. Through a last set of new, oak gates it reaches Weybourne Drive, which is followed back to the main road (A6). Here, the walk crosses the busy road on the pedestrian crossing and turns right, back to the pub.

③⓪ Whipsnade
The Old Hunters Lodge

Whipsnade is best known for the nearby Wild Animal Park, one of the largest conservation centres in Europe, which first opened as a zoo in 1931. The village is built around a village green and common land, with the Old Hunter's Lodge at its eastern end, next to one of the gates that once closed the road at night.

An attractive, thatched building, the oldest part of the Old Hunters Lodge is thought to date back to the 15th century whilst the newest is a restaurant extension built just a few years ago. Adjoining a small bar complete with ancient brick floor and low beams is a much larger room in which armchairs and settees around an open fire make a cosy setting for an informal, country bar. A choice of real ales is complemented by bar snacks and meals ranging from sandwiches and salads to pies, pastas and curries. On offer in the separate restaurant are such gastronomic delights as duck breast served in cherry liqueur sauce and fillet steak served flambé in brandy with green peppers and cream sauce. Sunday lunches are very popular and booking in advance is advisable. There is always a choice for vegetarians both in the bar and the restaurant. There is a garden and also a large patio for alfresco dining in warm weather.

The Old Hunters Lodge is a free house and currently serves three real ales: Greene King Abbott, Fuller's London Pride and Webster's Cask. Lager and cider are also available on draught. The opening times are Monday to Friday from 11.30 am to 2.30 pm and 6 pm to 11 pm. Saturday from 11.30 am to 3 pm and 6 pm to 11 pm and on Sunday from noon to 3 pm and 7 pm to 10.30 pm.
Telephone: (01582) 872228.

How to get there: Whipsnade is on the B4540, off the A5 (Dunstable–St Albans). Also easily reached from Dunstable town centre via the B4541 (follow the signs for Whipsnade Wild Animal Park). The Old Hunters Lodge is at the eastern end of the village.

Parking: There is a large car park to the left of the building.

Length of the walk: 4½ miles (short-cut available). OS map Landranger series 166 Luton, Hertford and surrounding area; Explorer 181 Chiltern Hills North. (Old Hunters Lodge GR 014181).

An exhilarating walk to Dunstable Downs with the highest views in Bedfordshire. En route there is a chance to explore the well-known Tree Cathedral and visit the Dunstable Downs Countryside Centre. In addition, gliders, hang-gliders, parascenders and kites taking advantage of the rising air along the line of the downs combine to create the most spectacular free show in the county.

The Walk
Across the road from the Old Hunters Lodge, a footpath is followed running to the right across the wide grass verge, part of the common land at this end of the village. The path runs parallel with the road and shortly passes the church of St Mary Magdalene which has a 16th century tower and some of the oldest brickwork in the county. Past the church the path keeps ahead to the village green where a waymark on a pole points right for the Tree Cathedral.

Now in company with the Icknield Way Path, the walk crosses over the main road and follows a road in front of cottages facing onto the green. Just past the last cottage, the route bears right along a track or driveway leading to the Tree Cathedral, still following the waymarks. Through a small car park and swing-gates, it bears left of the avenue of trees leading to the main entrance next to which, an information board gives full details of the Tree Cathedral. Now in the care of the National Trust it was originally planted by E. K. Blyth in the 1930s in memory of friends killed in World War I.

The path follows the Icknield Way Path waymarks to a stile over which it continues along the line of the fence behind the Dell Farm

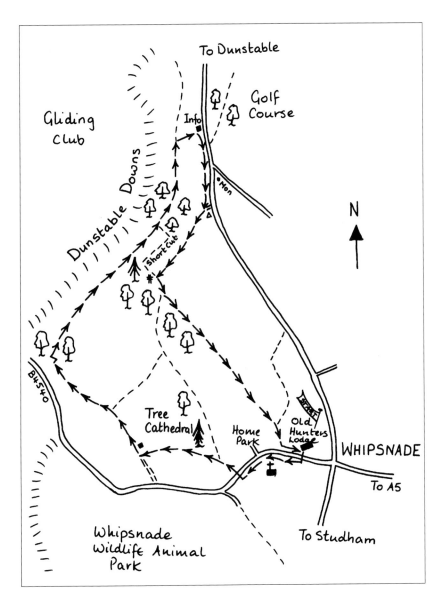

Residential Centre which organises rural studies for Bedfordshire schoolchildren. Within the Centre's grounds can usually be seen an interesting collection of rare breeds and semi-domesticated farm animals. Over another stile in the corner, the walk turns right on a wide track running past a bungalow. As it runs uphill, the track becomes more sunken and this stretch can be very muddy during winter months. At the top of the rise, a gap ahead reveals panoramic views across the plain below and along the line of the hills beyond Ivinghoe Beacon (see *Pub Walks Along the Icknield Way Path* by the author of this book).

Here, the walk bears right, then left, down through scrub to a track along which it turns right. Past a stile on the left and through a swing-gate, it continues ahead as the path crosses open hillside just below the brow of the escarpment. After a good distance, another swing-gate is reached at which point a short cut can be taken by turning right and following the path uphill – see sketch map. The main walk continues through the gate and follows the path ahead through a belt of scrub on the other side of which it keeps to the right of the bushes. From the Icknield Way information board, the path angles right across open hillside to the building which houses the Dunstable Downs Countryside Centre, a refreshment kiosk and toilets.

The Centre is open in the afternoons from April to September and at Bank Holidays and weekends throughout the year. From here, the walk parts company with the Icknield Way Path as the return route turns right, across the car park, keeping to the grass on a path running parallel to the road. As the emergency landing ground for gliders is crossed, a memorial on the other side of the road records that this land also was given to the National Trust in tribute to the memory of brothers who died fighting on the Western Front in World War I.

Beyond the short oak posts marking the emergency landing ground, the path runs ahead to a farm access road (just short of the trig point) along which it turns right. The road leads across open fields to a wood where the short cut rejoins the main walk as it comes in from the right. The walk leaves the road as it turns left, following the path as it runs along the edge of the wood. In front of the wireless telegraph mast, it forks left along a path which eventually clears the trees and then follows the line of a hedge before bearing right of a fence. The path becomes a hedged, sunken lane skirting one side of a mobile homes park before keeping ahead to reach open common land bordering the road just to the right of the Old Hunters Lodge.